Scott Foresman

Grade 1
Unit and End-of-Year
Benchmark Tests
Teacher's Manual

Glenview, Illinois • Boston, Massachusetts • Chandler, Arizona • Upper Saddle River, New Jersey

The Pearson Promise

As the largest educational publishing company in the world, Pearson is committed to providing you with curriculum that not only meets the Common Core State Standards, but also supports your implementation of these standards with your students.

Pearson has aligned the Common Core State Standards to every grade level of *Scott Foresman Reading Street*, our premier educational curriculum. This product provides an alignment of the Common Core State Standards to the Grade 1 assessment items in *Scott Foresman Reading Street Unit and End-of-Year Benchmark Tests*.

We value your partnership highly and look forward to continuing our mission to provide educational materials that fully satisfy your classroom needs.

ISBN-13: 978-0-328-68391-8
ISBN-10:   0-328-68391-4
5 6 7 8 9 10 V001 15 14 13 12

Contents

OVERVIEW

Scott Foresman *Reading Street* provides a wide array of formal tests and classroom assessments to support instruction. Formal assessments include the following:

- Baseline Group Tests

- Weekly Selection Tests

- Fresh Reads for Differentiated Test Practice

- Unit and End-of-Year Benchmark Tests aligned to Common Core State Standards

This Teacher's Manual provides information for administering the Benchmark Tests, scoring the tests, and interpreting the results. Detailed information about other assessment materials and procedures may be found in the *Assessment Handbook*.

Description of the Benchmark Tests

In Grade 1, there are six Unit Benchmark Tests—one for each unit—and an End-of-Year Test. The Unit Benchmark Tests are designed to measure a child's progress based on the comprehension skills and strategies, theme, types of writing, phonics skills, high-frequency words, and writing conventions taught in each unit. The End-of-Year Benchmark Test measures skills covered in all six units. The Benchmark Tests offer an integrated approach to assessment by measuring all skills and strategies in relation to reading selections.

In addition, the Benchmark Tests are designed to provide practice in test-taking skills and to prepare children to take the Reading/Language Arts section of standardized tests, state tests, or teacher-made tests. The tests include both multiple-choice and constructed-response questions. They also include writing prompts that will help children prepare for state writing tests.

Unit R Benchmark Test has these features:

- The content in Parts 1–6 of this test is based on targeted skills that review the Kindergarten units in these different areas:

Phonemic Awareness	Word Knowledge
Phonics	Comprehension
Word Reading	Writing

Units 1–5 Benchmark Tests have these features:

- Each test has two components—the Reading component (Parts 1–4) and the Writing component (Part 5).

- The Reading component (Parts 1–4) presents one or two selections. The genres of the selections, drawn from fiction and nonfiction, reflect the focus genres taught in each unit.

- Each selection reflects the theme of the unit.

- Each Reading component (Parts 1–4) of the tests for Units 1 and 2 contains forty multiple-choice questions. Each Reading component (Parts 1–4) of the tests for Units 3, 4, and 5 contains forty multiple-choice questions and two constructed-response questions. These questions test reading comprehension, literary skills and genre, critical-thinking skills, high-frequency words, phonics skills, and writing conventions. Some of the items measure the ability to synthesize information and to compare and contrast across texts.

- The Writing component (Part 5) of each test presents a writing prompt based on one of the types of writing taught in the unit. These prompts are similar to those found in state writing tests.

The End-of-Year Benchmark Test follows the same design as the Unit Benchmark Tests, but it has more items and a third selection. It measures selected skills from all six units taught during the year.

The Benchmark Tests are designed to assess a child's progress at the end of each unit and at the end of the school year. Selections and questions in the Unit Benchmark Tests become progressively more difficult from Unit R to Unit 5, to reflect the increasing sophistication of materials children are able to handle.

ADMINISTERING THE TESTS

The tasks in the Unit R Benchmark Test are designed to be administered to individuals, small groups, or the whole class, depending on the nature of each activity. Each task can be administered in one sitting. Units 1–5 Benchmark Tests are designed for group administration. You may decide to administer each test in one sitting, or you may administer parts of the test in two or more sittings. (For Units 3, 4, and 5, if you administer the test in two or more sittings, try to schedule the sittings on the same day or within a day of the previous sitting because some of the questions at the end of the test compare and contrast selections.)

These tests were also designed to give teachers the option of separating multiple-choice questions from the constructed-response questions. You may opt to remove or have children skip the constructed-response questions in order to create an all multiple-choice test.

These tests are not intended to be timed. We recommend allowing ample time for all children to complete the tests at their own pace. However, for the purposes

Unit	Test Part	Number of Items	Estimated Time
R	Phonemic Awareness – Part 1	13 multiple-choice items	20 minutes
	Phonics – Part 2	14 multiple-choice items	20–25 minutes
	Word Reading – Part 3	14 multiple-choice items	20 minutes
	Word Knowledge – Part 4	14 multiple-choice items	15 minutes
	Comprehension – Part 5	10 multiple-choice items	20–25 minutes
	Writing – Part 6 OPTIONAL	1 writing prompt	15–20 minutes
1-2	Reading – Part 1	14 multiple-choice items	20–25 minutes
	Reading – Part 2 (High-FrequencyWords)	6 multiple-choice items	8 minutes
	Reading – Part 3 (Phonics)	14 multiple-choice items	20–25 minutes
	Reading – Part 4 (Writing Conventions) OPTIONAL	6 multiple-choice items	8 minutes
	Writing – Part 5 OPTIONAL	1 writing prompt	15–20 minutes
3-5	Reading – Part 1 (Selection 1)	7 multiple choice items	10 minutes
		1 constructed-response item	5 minutes
	Reading – Part 1 (Selection 2)	7 multiple-choice items	10 minutes
		1 constructed-response item	5 minutes
	Reading – Part 2 (High-Frequency Words)	6 multiple-choice items	8 minutes
	Reading – Part 3 (Phonics)	14 multiple-choice items	20–25 minutes
	Reading – Part 4 (Writing Conventions) OPTIONAL	6 multiple-choice items	8 minutes
	Writing – Part 5 OPTIONAL	1 writing prompt	15–20 minutes

of scheduling, planning, and practicing timed-test situations, the chart shows the
number of items in each test part and the estimated amount of time required to
complete each section.

The End-of-Year Benchmark Test has three longer passages, sixty multiple-choice
items, two constructed-response items, and one writing prompt. To administer the
End-of-Year Benchmark Test, plan on about two hours for the Reading component
(Parts 1–4) and thirty minutes for the Writing component (Part 5).

Directions for Administering the Tests

Beginning on page T45 of this Teacher's Manual, you'll find specific directions for
administering each Unit Benchmark Test and the End-of-Year Benchmark Test.

Before you administer a test . . .

Review the test to familiarize yourself with the directions and the types of
questions. In the Reading component, children should mark their answers directly

on the test pages. In the Writing component, children will be drawing pictures or writing compositions in response to a writing prompt. They should write their responses on the lines provided in their tests. You may wish to provide scrap paper that children can use for planning their writing, but only the writing in their tests should be scored.

In Grade 1, the characteristics of the Benchmark Tests vary from unit to unit to match children's abilities to read the selections and handle directions. See the chart above for a description of each test. The directions below tell how the reading part of each test is intended to be administered. You may want to refer to these directions before administering the Reading component for each test.

Unit R Test, Reading Component (Parts 1–4)

Read all parts of the test aloud. Children circle the answer to each question.

Unit 1 Test, Reading Component (Parts 1–4)

Read all parts of the test—the selection and the questions—aloud. Children circle the answer to each question.

Unit 2 Test, Reading Component (Parts 1–4)

Children read the selection independently. If children cannot read independently, you may read them the selection. Read directions, questions, and answer choices aloud. Children mark their answers by filling in circles.

Unit 3 Test, Reading Component (Parts 1–4)

Children read the selections independently. Read directions and questions aloud. Children mark their answers by filling in circles or by writing the answer on the lines provided in their tests.

Unit 4 Test, Reading Component (Parts 1–4)

Children read the selections independently. Read directions and questions aloud. If appropriate, you may have children read the questions themselves. Children mark their answers by filling in circles or by writing the answer on the lines provided.

Unit 5 and End-of-Year Tests, Reading Component (Parts 1–4)

Children read the selections, questions, and answers independently. Read the directions aloud. Children mark their answers by filling in circles or by writing the answer on the lines provided in their tests.

When you are ready to administer a test . . .

Distribute a test to each child. Have children write their names on the front of their tests (and on any additional sheets of paper they may use). Hold up the test for children to see and have them flip through the test as you point out and explain its key features. For example, point out directions, selection titles, selections, art, Go

On and Stop symbols, multiple-choice questions with answer choices, constructed-response questions with lines for written answers, and the writing prompt with a checklist and lined pages for their compositions. Allow time for children to ask any questions they may have about the test's contents before you begin the test.

Follow the specific directions for each test beginning on page T45.

Directions in **bold** are to be read aloud; others are for your information only.

After testing . . .

Directions for scoring the test begin below. Answer keys begin on page T95. Evaluation Charts with alignments to Common Core State Standards (T29–T42) are provided along with a Class Record Chart on page T43.

SCORING THE TESTS

The Benchmark Tests for Units 1–5 are intended to be scored by part—a total score for the Reading component (Parts 1–4) and a separate score for the Writing component (Part 5). To make scoring easier, copy and use the following charts as needed:

- the Unit Benchmark Evaluation Charts, beginning on page T29, for recording a child's individual scores on a Unit Benchmark Test;

- the End-of-Year Benchmark Test Evaluation Chart, on pages T41 and T42, for recording a child's individual scores on the End-of-Year Benchmark Test;

- and the Class Record Chart, on page T43, for recording test scores for all children for all five units.

In Units R and 1, children mark their responses by circling a picture or word(s). The answer key for Unit 1 lists the complete response to each question.

In Unit 2, children fill in circles. The answer key for this unit lists the complete response to each question.

In Units 3–5 and in the End-of-Year test, children respond to multiple-choice questions by filling in circles. They also respond to constructed-response questions by writing their answers on lines provided in the tests. These two types of questions are scored in slightly different ways, as explained on pages T9–T10.

In all units, children respond to the writing prompt in the Writing component by writing (or drawing) a response. Each prompt is linked to one of four different types of writing: narrative, descriptive, expository, or persuasive. For each type of writing, there are four Writing Scoring Rubrics. Each rubric has a different point scale. Choose the rubric that most closely matches the rubrics used for your state's writing tests or the rubric that you deem most appropriate for your children. Writing Scoring Rubrics begin on page T11.

Scoring Multiple-Choice Questions

Each multiple-choice question has three answer choices. Refer to the answer key for the test you are scoring and mark each multiple-choice question correct (1 point) or incorrect (0 points).

Scoring Constructed-Response Questions

Children will respond to constructed-response questions beginning in Unit 3. Use the answer keys that begin on page T95 and the following rubric to help you score constructed-response questions. Award each constructed-response answer a score from 0 to 2 points, depending on how accurate and complete the response is. The answer keys provide abbreviated descriptions of top responses. Have an ideal top response in mind before you assess children's responses.

Constructed-Response Scoring Rubric

Points	Description
2	The response indicates a **full understanding** of the question's reading or critical-thinking skill. The response is accurate and complete. Necessary support and/or examples are included, and the information is clearly text-based.
1	The response indicates a **partial understanding** of the question's reading or critical-thinking skill. The response includes information that is essentially correct and text-based, but it is too general or too simplistic. Some of the support and/or examples may be incomplete or omitted.
0	The response is **inaccurate,** confused, and/or irrelevant, or the child has failed to respond to the task.

Scoring the Writing Component (Part 5)

The last part of each test requires children to draw pictures and/or write in response to a writing prompt. To evaluate children's written responses to a writing prompt, familiarize yourself with the writing prompt and review the Writing Scoring Rubrics on pages T11–T18. Identify the type of writing suggested in the writing prompt. (Types of writing for each prompt are identified in the answer keys that begin on page T95.) Then choose one of the four Writing Scoring Rubrics provided for that type of writing. Use the rubric to score each composition on a scale from 1 to 6, 1 to 5, 1 to 4, or 1 to 3.

Writing Scoring Rubrics: Narrative Writing

6-Point Scoring Rubric

6	5	4	3	2	1
narrative writing is well focused on the topic	narrative writing is focused on the topic	narrative writing is generally focused on the topic	narrative writing is generally focused but may stray from the topic	narrative writing is minimally related to the topic	narrative writing is not focused on the topic
contains clear ideas	most ideas are clear	ideas are generally clear	ideas may be somewhat unclear	ideas are often unclear	ideas are unclear
logically organized; uses transitions	logically organized; uses some transitions	logically organized with some lapses; has transitions	somewhat organized; may lack transitions	minimally organized; no transitions	unorganized; no transitions
voice is engaging; well suited to purpose and audience	voice comes through well; suited to purpose and audience	voice comes through occasionally; suited to purpose and audience	voice uneven; not always suited to purpose or audience	slight evidence of voice; little sense of purpose or audience	weak voice; no sense of purpose or audience
demonstrates varied, precise word choice	generally demonstrates varied, precise word choice	often demonstrates varied, precise word choice	word choice could be more varied, precise	poor choice of words; limited vocabulary	limited vocabulary
sentences are complete, fluent, and varied	most sentences are complete and varied	many sentences are complete and varied	some incomplete sentences; little variety	sentences are incomplete; show little or no variety	gross errors in sentence structure; no variety
shows excellent control of writing conventions	shows very good control of writing conventions	shows good control of writing conventions	shows fair control of writing conventions	shows frequent errors in writing conventions	shows many serious errors in writing conventions

5-Point Scoring Rubric

5	4	3	2	1
narrative writing is well focused on the topic	narrative writing is focused on the topic	narrative writing is generally focused on the topic	narrative writing strays from the topic	narrative writing is not focused on the topic
contains clear ideas	most ideas are clear	ideas are generally clear	many ideas are unclear	ideas are unclear
logically organized; uses transitions	logically organized; uses some transitions	logically organized with some lapses; transitions weak	little organization; few or no transitions	unorganized; no transitions
voice is engaging; well suited to purpose and audience	voice is fairly strong; suited to purpose and audience	voice comes through occasionally; may not suit purpose or audience	voice comes through rarely; poorly suited to purpose or audience	weak voice; no sense of audience or purpose
demonstrates varied, precise word choice	generally demonstrates varied, precise word choice	word choice could be more varied, precise	poor choice of words; limited vocabulary	choice of words very limited
sentences are complete, fluent, and varied	most sentences are complete and varied	many sentences are complete; generally varied	incomplete sentences; little variety	incomplete sentences; no variety
shows excellent control of writing conventions	shows very good control of writing conventions	shows fairly good control of writing conventions	shows frequent errors in writing conventions	shows many serious errors in writing conventions

Writing Scoring Rubrics: Narrative Writing

4-Point Scoring Rubric

4	3	2	1
narrative writing is well focused on the topic	narrative writing is focused on the topic	narrative writing may stray from the topic	narrative writing is not focused on the topic
contains clear ideas	most ideas are clear	some ideas may be unclear	ideas are unclear
logically organized; uses transitions	logically organized; uses some transitions	little organization; may be few or no transitions	unorganized; no transitions
voice is engaging; well suited to purpose and audience	voice is fairly strong; suited to purpose and audience	slight evidence of voice; may be poorly suited to purpose or audience	weak voice; no sense of audience or purpose
demonstrates varied, precise word choice	generally demonstrates varied, precise word choice	choice of words limited	choice of words very limited
sentences are complete, fluent, and varied	most sentences are complete and varied	many incomplete sentences; little variety	mostly incomplete sentences; no variety
shows excellent control of writing conventions	shows very good control of writing conventions	shows frequent errors in writing conventions	shows many serious errors in writing conventions

3-Point Scoring Rubric

3	2	1
narrative writing is well focused on the topic	narrative writing is generally focused on the topic	narrative writing is not focused on the topic
contains clear ideas	ideas are sometimes unclear	ideas are unclear
logically organized; uses transitions	logically organized with lapses; transitions need improvement	unorganized; no transitions
voice is engaging; well suited to purpose and audience	voice comes through fairly well; may not suit purpose or audience	weak voice; no sense of audience
demonstrates varied, precise word choice	word choice could be more varied, precise	choice of words very limited
sentences are complete, fluent, and varied	some sentences are complete and varied	incomplete sentences; no variety
shows excellent control of writing conventions	shows fair control of writing conventions	shows many serious errors in writing conventions

Writing Scoring Rubrics: Descriptive Writing

6-Point Scoring Rubric

6	5	4	3	2	1
descriptive writing is well focused on the topic	descriptive writing is focused on the topic	descriptive writing is generally focused on the topic	descriptive writing may stray from the topic	descriptive writing is minimally related to the topic	descriptive writing is not focused on the topic
contains clear ideas	most ideas are clear	ideas are generally clear	ideas may be somewhat unclear	ideas are often unclear	ideas are unclear
logically organized; uses transitions	logically organized; uses some transitions	logically organized with some lapses; has transitions	somewhat organized; may lack transitions	minimally organized; no transitions	unorganized; no transitions
voice is engaging; well suited to purpose and audience	voice comes through well; suited to purpose and audience	voice comes through occasionally; suited to purpose and audience	voice uneven; not always suited to purpose or audience	slight evidence of voice; little sense of purpose or audience	weak voice; no sense of purpose or audience
precise, vivid language paints strong pictures	generally demonstrates varied, precise word choice	often demonstrates varied, precise word choice	word choice could be more varied, precise	poor choice of words; limited vocabulary	limited vocabulary
sentences are complete, fluent, and varied	most sentences are complete and varied	many sentences are complete and varied	some incomplete sentences; little variety	sentences are incomplete; show little or no variety	gross errors in sentence structure; no variety
shows excellent control of writing conventions	shows very good control of writing conventions	shows good control of writing conventions	shows fair control of writing conventions	shows frequent errors in writing conventions	shows many serious errors in writing conventions

5-Point Scoring Rubric

5	4	3	2	1
descriptive writing is well focused on the topic	descriptive writing is focused on the topic	descriptive writing is generally focused on the topic	descriptive writing strays from the topic	descriptive writing is not focused on the topic
contains clear ideas	most ideas are clear	ideas are generally clear	many ideas are unclear	ideas are unclear
logically organized; uses transitions	logically organized; uses some transitions	logically organized with some lapses; transitions weak	little organization; few or no transitions	unorganized; no transitions
voice is engaging; well suited to purpose and audience	voice is fairly engaging; suited to purpose and audience	voice comes through occasionally; may not suit purpose or audience	voice comes through rarely; poorly suited to purpose or audience	weak voice; no sense of audience or purpose
demonstrates varied, precise word choice	generally demonstrates varied, precise word choice	word choice could be more varied, precise	poor word choice; limited vocabulary	word choice very limited
sentences are complete, fluent, and varied	most sentences are complete and varied	many sentences are complete; generally varied	incomplete sentences; little variety	incomplete sentences; no variety
shows excellent control of writing conventions	shows very good control of writing conventions	shows fairly good control of writing conventions	shows frequent errors in writing conventions	shows many serious errors in writing conventions

Writing Scoring Rubrics: Descriptive Writing

4-Point Scoring Rubric

4	3	2	1
descriptive writing is well focused on the topic	descriptive writing is focused on the topic	descriptive writing may stray from the topic	descriptive writing is not focused on the topic
contains clear ideas	most ideas are clear	some ideas may be unclear	ideas are unclear
logically organized; uses transitions	logically organized; uses some transitions	little organization; may be few or no transitions	unorganized; no transitions
voice is engaging; well suited to purpose and audience	voice is fairly engaging; suited to purpose and audience	slight evidence of voice; may be poorly suited to audience or purpose	weak voice; no sense of audience or purpose
demonstrates varied, precise word choice	generally demonstrates varied, precise word choice	choice of words limited	word choice very limited
sentences are complete, fluent, and varied	most sentences are complete and varied	many incomplete sentences; little variety	mostly incomplete sentences; no variety
shows excellent control of writing conventions	shows very good control of writing conventions	shows frequent errors in writing conventions	shows many serious errors in writing conventions

3-Point Scoring Rubric

3	2	1
descriptive writing is well focused on the topic	descriptive writing is generally focused on the topic	descriptive writing is not focused on the topic
contains clear ideas	ideas are sometimes unclear	ideas are unclear
logically organized; uses transitions	logically organized with lapses; transitions need improvement	unorganized; no transitions
voice is engaging; well suited to purpose and audience	voice comes through fairly well; may not suit purpose or audience	weak voice; no sense of purpose or audience
demonstrates varied, precise word choice	word choice could be more varied, precise	choice of words very limited
sentences are complete, fluent, and varied	some sentences are complete and varied	incomplete sentences; no variety
shows excellent control of writing conventions	shows fair control of writing conventions	shows many serious errors in writing conventions

Writing Scoring Rubrics: Expository Writing

6-Point Scoring Rubric

6	5	4	3	2	1
expository writing is well focused on the topic	expository writing is focused on the topic	expository writing is generally focused on the topic	expository writing may stray from the topic	expository writing is minimally related to the topic	expository writing is not focused on the topic
contains clear ideas	most ideas are clear	ideas are generally clear	ideas may be somewhat unclear	ideas are often unclear	ideas are unclear
logically organized; uses transitions	logically organized; uses some transitions	logically organized with some lapses; has transitions	little organization; may lack transitions	minimally organized; no transitions	unorganized; no transitions
voice is engaging; well suited to purpose and audience	voice comes through well; suited to purpose and audience	voice comes through occasionally; suited to purpose and audience	voice uneven; not always suited to purpose or audience	slight evidence of voice; little sense of purpose or audience	weak voice; no sense of purpose or audience
demonstrates varied, precise word choice	generally demonstrates varied, precise word choice	often demonstrates varied, precise word choice	word choice could be more varied, precise	poor choice of words; limited vocabulary	limited vocabulary
sentences are complete, fluent, and varied	most sentences are complete and varied	many sentences are complete and varied	some incomplete sentences; little variety	sentences are incomplete; show little or no variety	gross errors in sentence structure; no variety
shows excellent control of writing conventions	shows very good control of writing conventions	shows good control of writing conventions	shows fair control of writing conventions	shows frequent errors in writing conventions	shows many serious errors in writing conventions

5-Point Scoring Rubric

5	4	3	2	1
expository writing is well focused on the topic	expository writing is focused on the topic	expository writing is generally focused on the topic	expository writing strays from the topic	expository writing is not focused on the topic
contains clear ideas	most ideas are clear	ideas are generally clear	many ideas are unclear	ideas are unclear
logically organized; uses transitions	logically organized; uses some transitions	logically organized with some lapses; transitions weak	little organization; few or no transitions	unorganized; no transitions
voice is engaging; well suited to purpose and audience	voice is fairly engaging; suited to purpose and audience	voice comes through occasionally; may not suit purpose or audience	voice comes through rarely; poorly suited to purpose or audience	weak voice; no sense of audience or purpose
demonstrates varied, precise word choice	generally demonstrates varied, precise word choice	word choice could be more varied, precise	poor word choice; limited vocabulary	word choice very limited
sentences are complete, fluent, and varied	most sentences are complete and varied	many sentences are complete; generally varied	incomplete sentences; little variety	incomplete sentences; no variety
shows excellent control of writing conventions	shows very good control of writing conventions	shows fairly good control of writing conventions	shows frequent errors in writing conventions	shows many serious errors in writing conventions

Writing Scoring Rubrics: Expository Writing

4-Point Scoring Rubric

4	3	2	1
expository writing is well focused on the topic	expository writing is focused on the topic	expository writing may stray from the topic	expository writing is not focused on the topic
contains clear ideas	most ideas are clear	some ideas may be unclear	ideas are unclear
logically organized; uses transitions	logically organized; uses some transitions	little organization; may be few or no transitions	unorganized; no transitions
voice is engaging; well suited to purpose and audience	voice is fairly engaging; suited to purpose and audience	slight evidence of voice; may be poorly suited to audience or purpose	weak voice; no sense of audience or purpose
demonstrates varied, precise word choice	generally demonstrates varied, precise word choice	choice of words limited	word choice very limited
sentences are complete, fluent, and varied	most sentences are complete and varied	many incomplete sentences; little variety	mostly incomplete sentences; no variety
shows excellent control of writing conventions	shows very good control of writing conventions	shows frequent errors in writing conventions	shows many serious errors in writing conventions

3-Point Scoring Rubric

3	2	1
expository writing is well focused on the topic	expository writing is generally focused on the topic	expository writing is not focused on the topic
contains clear ideas	ideas are sometimes unclear	ideas are unclear
logically organized; uses transitions	logically organized with lapses; transitions need improvement	unorganized; no transitions
voice is engaging; well suited to purpose and audience	voice comes through fairly well; may not suit purpose or audience	weak voice; no sense of purpose or audience
demonstrates varied, precise word choice	word choice could be more varied, precise	choice of words very limited
sentences are complete, fluent, and varied	some sentences are complete and varied	incomplete sentences; no variety
shows excellent control of writing conventions	shows fair control of writing conventions	shows many serious errors in writing conventions

Writing Scoring Rubrics: Persuasive Writing

6-Point Scoring Rubric

6	5	4	3	2	1
persuasive writing is well focused on the topic	persuasive writing is focused on the topic	persuasive writing is generally focused on the topic	persuasive writing is generally focused but may stray from the topic	persuasive writing is minimally related to the topic	persuasive writing is not focused on the topic
contains clear ideas	most ideas are clear	ideas are generally clear	ideas may be somewhat unclear	ideas are often unclear	ideas are unclear
presents reasons in order; uses transitions	presents reasons in some order; uses some transitions	presents most reasons in order; has transitions	reasons may not be in proper order; may lack transitions	reasons are not in order; no transitions	reasons, if any, are not in order; no transitions
voice is engaging; well suited to purpose and audience	voice comes through well; suited to purpose and audience	voice comes through occasionally; suited to purpose and audience	voice uneven; not always suited to purpose or audience	slight evidence of voice; little sense of audience or purpose	weak voice; no sense of purpose or audience
demonstrates precise, persuasive wording	generally demonstrates precise, persuasive word choice	often demonstrates precise, persuasive word choice	word choice is not always precise or persuasive	poor choice of words; not very persuasive	limited vocabulary; fails to persuade
sentences are complete, fluent, and varied	most sentences are complete and varied	many sentences are complete and varied	some incomplete sentences; little variety	sentences are incomplete; show little or no variety	gross errors in sentence structure; no variety
shows excellent control of writing conventions	shows very good control of writing conventions	shows good control of writing conventions	shows fair control of writing conventions	shows frequent errors in writing conventions	shows many serious errors in writing conventions

5-Point Scoring Rubric

5	4	3	2	1
persuasive writing is well focused on the topic	persuasive writing is focused on the topic	persuasive writing is generally focused on the topic	persuasive writing strays from the topic	persuasive writing is not focused on the topic
contains clear ideas	most ideas are clear	ideas are generally clear	many ideas are unclear	ideas are unclear
presents reasons in order; uses transitions	presents reasons in some order; uses some transitions	presents most reasons in order; transitions weak	reasons are not in order; few or no transitions	reasons, if any, are not in order; no transitions
voice is engaging; well suited to purpose and audience	voice is fairly engaging; suited to purpose and audience	voice comes through occasionally; may not suit purpose or audience	voice comes through rarely; poorly suited to audience or purpose	weak voice; no sense of audience or purpose
demonstrates precise, persuasive wording	generally demonstrates precise, persuasive word choice	word choice could be more precise, persuasive	word choice limited; not persuasive	word choice very limited; fails to persuade
sentences are complete, fluent, and varied	most sentences are complete and varied	many sentences are complete; generally varied	incomplete sentences; little variety	incomplete sentences; no variety
shows excellent control of writing conventions	shows very good control of writing conventions	shows fairly good control of writing conventions	shows frequent errors in writing conventions	shows many serious errors in writing conventions

■ ■

Writing Scoring Rubrics: Persuasive Writing

4-Point Scoring Rubric

4	3	2	1
persuasive writing is well focused on the topic	persuasive writing is focused on the topic	persuasive writing may stray from the topic	persuasive writing is not focused on the topic
contains clear ideas	most ideas are clear	some ideas may be unclear	ideas are unclear
presents reasons in order; uses transitions	presents reasons in some order; uses some transitions	reasons may not be in order; may be few or no transitions	reasons, if any, are not in order; no transitions
voice is engaging; well suited to purpose and audience	voice is fairly engaging; suited to purpose and audience	slight evidence of voice; may be poorly suited to purpose or audience	weak voice; no sense of audience or purpose
demonstrates precise, persuasive wording	generally demonstrates precise, persuasive word choice	choice of words limited; not very persuasive	word choice very limited; fails to persuade
sentences are complete, fluent, and varied	most sentences are complete and varied	many incomplete sentences; little variety	many incomplete sentences; no variety
shows excellent control of writing conventions	shows very good control of writing conventions	shows frequent errors in writing conventions	shows many serious errors in writing conventions

3-Point Scoring Rubric

3	2	1
persuasive writing is well focused on the topic	persuasive writing is generally focused on the topic	persuasive writing is not focused on the topic
contains clear ideas	ideas are sometimes unclear	ideas are unclear
logically organized; presents reasons in order	logically organized with lapses; presents most reasons in order	unorganized; reasons, if any, are not in order
voice is engaging; well suited to purpose and audience	voice comes through fairly well; may not suit audience or purpose	weak voice; no sense of audience or purpose
demonstrates precise, persuasive word choice	word choice could be more precise, persuasive	choice of words very limited; fails to persuade
sentences are complete, fluent, and varied	some sentences are complete and varied	incomplete sentences; no variety
shows excellent control of writing conventions	shows fair control of writing conventions	shows many serious errors in writing conventions

Using an Evaluation Chart

Use the Evaluation Charts on pages T29 through T42 to score the Unit Benchmark Tests and the End-of-Year Benchmark Test. To score one of these tests using an Evaluation Chart, use the following procedure:

1. Make a copy of the appropriate Evaluation Chart for each child.

2. To score Reading – Parts 1–4 (or 5 for Unit R), circle the score for each item on the Evaluation Chart. Multiple-choice questions are scored 0 or 1 point (incorrect or correct). Constructed-response questions are scored 0, 1, or 2 points, depending on how accurate and complete the response is. Use the answer key for the test you are scoring and the Constructed-Response Scoring Rubric on page T10 to help you score Reading – Parts 1–4 (or 5 for Unit R).

3. Find the child's total score for Reading – Parts 1–4 (or 5 for Unit R) by adding the individual scores for all items.

4. For Units 1–5 use the formula on the Evaluation Chart to find the percentage score for Reading – Parts 1–4 by dividing the total *obtained* score by the total *possible* score and then multiplying the quotient by 100.

5. To score Writing – Part 5 (or 6 for Unit R), identify the type of writing suggested in the prompt, and choose one of the four Writing Scoring Rubrics for that type of writing. Read the child's writing and score each composition on a scale from 1 to 6, 1 to 5, 1 to 4, or 1 to 3.

6. Mark the child's writing score on the Evaluation Chart. Add any notes or observations about the writing that may be helpful to you and the child in later instruction.

INTERPRETING TEST RESULTS

A child's score on a Benchmark Test provides only one look at the child's progress and should be interpreted in conjunction with other assessments and the teacher's observations. However a low score on one or both parts of a Benchmark Test probably indicates a need for closer review of the child's performance and perhaps additional instruction.

Regrouping for Instruction

The Benchmark Tests can help you make regrouping decisions. In Grade 1 there are opportunities for regrouping at the end of Units 1, 2, 3, and 4. Depending on each child's progress, teachers may prefer to regroup more or less frequently.

Children who score 65% or below on the multiple-choice items of the Comprehension, High-Frequency Words, and Phonics sections of the Benchmark Tests and who typically demonstrate unsatisfactory work on assignments and in classroom discussions would benefit from being in the Strategic Intervention reading group for the next unit of instruction.

Children who score between 66% and 90% on the multiple-choice items of the Comprehension, High-Frequency Words, and Phonics sections of the Benchmark

Tests and who meet other criteria, such as consistently satisfactory work on assignments and in classroom discussions, likely belong in the On-Level reading group for the next unit of instruction. Children in the low end of that range should be observed carefully and may need on-going assistance, extra instruction, and opportunities for further practice, just as children in the Strategic Intervention group do. Children in the upper end of that range should receive their instruction and practice with on-level materials, but they may need extra challenge and enrichment, just as children in the Advanced reading group do.

Children who score 91% or above on the multiple-choice items of the Comprehension, High-Frequency Words, and Phonics sections of the Benchmark Tests and who meet other criteria, such as consistently excellent performance on assigned paperwork and in classroom discussions, are capable of work in the Advanced reading group for the next unit of instruction. They should be given multiple opportunities to engage in enrichment activities and real-world investigations.

Further Analysis of Results

Each Reading – Parts 1–4 (and 5 for Unit R) item on an Evaluation Chart is linked to a tested skill and a Common Core State Standard. Identifying which items the child answered incorrectly and referring to the list of tested skills may indicate specific skills or areas in which the child needs additional help. For example, if the child answers six questions incorrectly and several involve literary elements such as plot and character, you may want to plan additional instruction for the child in this area. While the Benchmark Tests do not provide sufficient content coverage of individual skills to be truly "diagnostic," children's performance patterns can often provide useful clues as to particular strengths and weaknesses.

Grading: For more information on how to use a writing assessment scale as an element of classroom grades, refer to the "Grading Writing" section of the *Assessment Handbook*.

ASSISTING ENGLISH LANGUAGE LEARNERS

While the Benchmark Tests provide teachers with a way to measure children's progress on a unit-by-unit basis, Benchmark Tests also provide an opportunity for teachers to help English language learners become familiar with the linguistic patterns and structures they will encounter while taking state tests. The format of the Benchmark Tests is similar to the format of the state tests, with similar direction lines, question stems, answer formats, and markings to "stop" and "go on."

Among assessment tools, standardized tests cause teachers of English language learners the most concern. State tests, considered "high stakes," may be used to evaluate the effectiveness of the curriculum, the teacher, or the instructional approach. They are used to evaluate children's overall progress. High-stakes tests are typically designed and normed for proficient speakers of English. By providing opportunities for children to become familiar with the formats and language of the Benchmark Tests, teachers assist English Language Learners in obtaining results that reflect children's learning of the content rather than their aptitude for comprehending test language and formats. Teachers can use specific strategies to prepare English language learners for assessment. Using these strategies on the Benchmark Tests will increase children's comfort levels and success with assessment tools such as the state tests.

Testing Strategies for All English Language Learners

Provide Accommodations for Children's Success

Any accommodations appropriate for English language learners should address children's linguistic needs, either directly or indirectly. As you consider accommodations for children taking the Benchmark Tests, remember that when the state tests are given, no special accommodations are allowed. Therefore, as you make accommodations for English language learners, keep in mind that the ultimate goal is for these children to handle mainstream testing settings, terminology, and instruction, so any accommodations that you provide should be considered stepping stones to children's eventual successful encounter with mainstream testing conditions.

1. **Simplify and clarify directions.** Providing instructions in simplified formats can reduce the language load for English language learners and help them focus solely on the task and content for the specific question(s). A good rule of thumb is to match the language used with the test to the language used with instruction. It is helpful to children when you replace complex English words with simpler English words that they are already familiar with or can grasp more easily. However, it is never appropriate to translate test directions into children's first languages. This practice will not benefit children when they encounter state tests. (*See below* **A Word of Caution**.) However, you may ask children to restate directions in their own words so you are sure they understand them.

2. **Provide a setting consistent with the instructional setting.** Administering tests in an alternate, smaller, even one-to-one, setting can allow for verbal scaffolding and provide English language learners with a setting that is comfortable and familiar to them. Be sure that the alternate setting is a setting with which children are familiar. Move children to mainstream testing settings as soon as they are ready.

3. **Consider timing.** Provide additional testing time and allow frequent or extended breaks during testing. On the Benchmark Tests, for example, children may benefit from a break between the two Comprehension selection/item sets or after the Comprehension section and before the High-Frequency Words section. The Writing sections are rigorous for children. Consider completing these portions on a different day or after a significant break. Keep in mind, however, that while this type of accommodation is one that is most often used for English language learners in mainstream classrooms, it is more important to be sure that children are receiving the necessary linguistic support in English.

4. **Provide dictionaries.** Allow the use of bilingual, word-for-word translation dictionaries as an accommodation for children who are able to use them effectively.

5. **Read aloud repeatedly.** Read the test selections orally as often as necessary in the Unit R and Unit 1 Benchmark Tests when listening comprehension is being assessed.

A Word of Caution: In providing accommodations to children, it is important not to compromise the intent of the assessment. It is never appropriate to read aloud the reading comprehension selections or the vocabulary and writing conventions questions unless directions specifically call for reading these portions aloud. Similarly, it is never appropriate to translate high-frequency words and phonics questions or comprehension selections and questions into children's native languages. These practices alter the constructs of the assessments. For example, the reading comprehension assessments are designed to measure both word recognition and understanding, so reading the selections to children actually changes the intent of the tests.

Following the administration of the assessments, it is important to note which accommodations were used for English language learners and to interpret scores with that information in mind. As children progress in their English language skills and become more comfortable with testing, it is important to reconsider accommodations that were given on previous tests.

Familiarize Children with Academic Language and Test Language

The Benchmark Tests use routine terminology and formats that are designed to mirror the experience of taking the state tests. Helping children improve their understanding and use of academic language is an essential way to prepare children for assessment. The practice of "teaching to the test" is often criticized—and rightfully so—but helping children understand the language of tests and other assessment instruments levels the playing field for English language learners, allowing them to demonstrate what they've learned about the content, rather than struggling with the test language and formats. All children, but especially English language learners, must be taught test-taking strategies and must build background about the language and procedures of taking tests. What strategies can you explicitly offer to children to prepare for assessment?

1. Focus on Academic English and Meaningful Oral Language Experiences

Many English language learners may quickly master *social* English, the conversational language skills and conventions used in everyday interactions with classmates. These same learners, however, frequently encounter difficulty with the *academic* English found on formal assessments. Children may also have gaps in understanding between oral and written English. The structure of academic English is complex, e.g., fiction and nonfiction text structures, paragraph organization, and syntax, including prepositional phrases, introductory clauses, and pronoun references. There are structural analysis constraints at the word, sentence, paragraph, and text levels.

Benchmark Tests Teacher's Manual

Development of academic language is one of the primary sources of difficulty for English language learners at all ages and grades while also being fundamental to all children's success. The vocabulary of academic English consists of specialized meanings of common words, abstract concepts, multiple-meaning words, and words based on Latin and Greek roots. As children read test selections, they may encounter unfamiliar topics and concepts. Recognize that it takes years for children to master academic English, but that you can help them make progress on the way. Highlight and discuss routinely the *academic* language, vocabulary, syntax, and narrative and expository text structures encountered in textbooks and trade books. Remember that academic English is not another name for "standard English." Academic English is the special form of English that is used in the classroom and in written texts. The grammatical constructions, words, and rhetorical conventions are not often used in everyday spoken language. The home language does *not* have to be English in order for children to benefit from experiences in using academic language. If it proves helpful, children may be encouraged to connect what they know in their home languages to what they are learning about academic English.

Provide children with experiences with academic language by reading to them and discussing readings, instructional activities, and experiences. Draw children into instructional conversations focused on the language they encounter in their school texts and other materials to show children how language works. Provide children with ample opportunities to use the language of texts—and tests—in speaking and in writing. Provide regular opportunities for meaningful oral language experiences in which English language learners participate in discussion of important topics and perform the activities required on tests, such as explaining, describing, comparing, and stating and supporting opinions. Encourage them to use vocabulary that will support academic language development in increased opportunities for structured academic talk.

2. Focus on Test Directions

Help children understand verbal phrases, such as "follow along," "draw a circle around," "listen for," "move down to the next row," and "fill in the circle," that are often used in test directions. When possible, model tasks and provide verbal directions in simpler, more common English words. Be explicit in your teaching, using the following examples to guide you.

> **Move down to the next row where you see the square.**
> **Put your finger on it.**

For the directions above, talk about the phrase "move down." Be sure that children understand that they need to *go to* the *next* row of pictures. Model and gesture how to follow these directions.

> **Circle the word** *green . . . green.*

For the directions above, model and explain how to *draw a circle around* one word in a row of three words. Be sure that children understand how to do this clearly and neatly.

> **Fill in the circle beside your answer.**

For the directions above, talk about the phrase "fill in" and the word "beside." Model and gesture how to follow the directions: *I use this page. I find the number of the question. I read the answers. Then I find the circle next to the correct answer and make it dark, or black, with my pencil.* Be sure children understand how to follow these directions clearly and neatly.

3. Focus on Terminology and Strategies

Think about terms that will make the most sense to children as you teach. Instead of using the words "directions," "test," and "fill in," for example, you might use common cognates such as *instructions*, *exam*, and *mark*, which translate to most Romance languages (i.e., in Spanish: *instrucciones*, *examen*, and *marca*). Instead of using the prepositions "by" and "beside" in phrases such as "by the star," and "beside the square," you might use the more common preposition *next to*. However, move children to the original test words as soon as possible.

Preteach the "language of tests" encountered in directions and test items, including:

> Question words, such as: *who, what, which, where, when, why, how,* and *what kind*
> Shape words, such as: *circle, diamond, heart, oval, rectangle, square, star,* and *triangle*
> Place words, such as: *bottom, top, above, below, over, under, up,* and *down*
> Sequence words and phrases, such as: *before, after, first, next, last, then, now, beginning, middle, ending,* and *all day long*
> Grammatical words and phrases, such as: *adjective, noun, pronoun, verb, sentence,* and *question*
> Descriptive verbs, such as: *look like, feel like, make feel,* and *make happy*
> Action verbs, such as: *draw, circle, tell, describe, rhyme, show,* and *write.*

Words such as *both* and *not* may seem simple, but their uses in test questions often prove otherwise. English language learners need help in seeing how such words frame and constrain ideas expressed in sentences in which they appear.

Throughout the year, children need robust vocabulary instruction in English for additional common test words and phrases, such as *test form, test booklet, author, selection, written composition, writing prompt, base your answer on, sentence, question, details, tell, describe, explain,* and *statement of fact* or *opinion.*

Examine the tests for other words and phrases that are important for children to learn.

Familiarize children with basic test formats, such as multiple-choice (3 options) and constructed-response items, cloze sentences, underlining of key words and sounds, and writing prompts for written compositions, so that they develop skills in locating key information. Be explicit in your teaching, using the following examples to guide you. Use released tests or models of tests, providing children with plenty of practice in test formats. Be aware that Units R and 1 tests have various picture and letter or word formats that are a carryover from the Kindergarten tests.

PHONEMIC AWARENESS

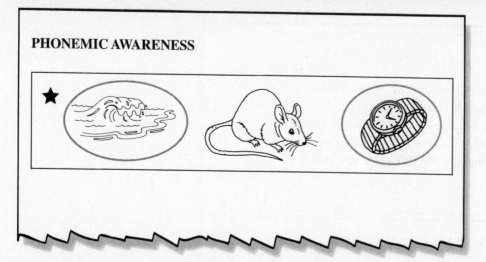

Explain the format: *Some tests have rows of pictures. There are small, black shapes at the beginning of each row. The teacher will tell me to go to a shape. Put my finger on it. Look at the three pictures next to it. Two words begin with the same sound. One word begins with a different sound. The teacher will ask me to draw a circle around the two pictures of words that begin with the same sound.* Model and gesture how to follow these directions. Be sure that children understand how to do this clearly and neatly.

---

15 **Which word makes this sentence correct?**
The dog can not _____ his bone.

○   family

○   some

○   find

Explain the test format: *On some tests, there are sentences with a line. The line shows a word is missing in the sentence. I need to choose the word that fits in the sentence the best. This is the word that makes the sentence sound correct.*

---

21 **Lee and Pam play in the park.**
Which word rhymes with play?

○   stay

○   back

○   math

Explain the test format: *Sometimes, tests have words that are underlined. That means a line is under the word. I pay special attention to words with lines under them. Questions ask about these words. In this test, the words with lines under them have special sounds.*

PROMPT

In "The Hale Boys Build a Car" and "Riding a Horse," children become old enough to do something new. Think about something new that you have learned to do this year. Write a story about a new thing you did this year. Tell how it made you feel.

CHECKLIST FOR WRITERS

_____ Did I plan my story before I started writing?

_____ Does my story tell about something new I learned to do this year?

_____ Does my story tell how doing something new made me feel?

_____ Does my story have a beginning, middle, and end?

_____ Does my story make sense?

_____ Do my sentences begin with capital letters?

_____ Do my sentences end with end marks?

_____ Did I check my spelling?

_____ Did I make sure my paper is the way I want readers to read it?

Explain the test format: *Some tests ask me to write a composition, or story. At the top of the page is an instruction box, or writing prompt. I read the instructions in the box to learn what to write about. There is one page of lines for me to write on.* Explain also the checklist box: *These are questions I read to myself and answer as I check over my writing to make sure it's just the way I want it.*

Explain the test format: *Some tests have stories. The stories are long. They will not fit on one page. This sign says "Go on." That means that I need to go to the next page and read more.*

Explain the test format: *Some test pages have this sign at the bottom. This sign says "Stop." That means it is the end of the test. I do not go to the next page until the teacher tells me to do that.*

Model test-taking strategies for children. Help them use their emerging familiarity with high-frequency words and basic language structures in English to choose the best answer and eliminate incorrect answer choices. Teach children the logic of test questions. Show children, for example, that the question "Which of the following is *not* a sentence?" means that all of the answer choices except one *are* sentences. Be sure to teach children the various types of reading comprehension questions they may encounter on tests, such as main idea and author's purpose. Use released test items or models of test items to provide children with plenty of practice in various question types and the test-taking strategies you have taught them.

---

1   **What did people chew for <u>gum</u> in the <u>past</u>?**

○   trees

○   sap

○   sticks

Model a test-taking strategy for children—underlining key words in the question: *I read the whole story carefully before I try to answer the questions. What do I do if I can't remember something? Do I guess? No. I can make lines under the important words in the question. Then I can go back and look for these words in the selection. I can read parts of the selection again. This will help me find the correct answer.*

---

14   **What *best* tells about Joy?**

○   She hopes that drawing pictures will make her rich.

○   She is tired of spending time with Dan.

○   She can have fun even on a rainy day.

Model a test-taking strategy for children—eliminating incorrect answer choices: *I read the whole story carefully before I try to answer the questions. This question asks about the main character, or most important person in the story. First, I think about what I remember about Joy. I can look at the story again where her name is and read again about her. I can look at the picture to help me too. What is Joy like? What does she like to do? What did she do in this story? Now I read the answer choices. I try to cross out two answers that do not match the story. The story does not say anything about Joy wanting to be rich, so that is not the correct answer. In the picture, Joy looks happy, so the second answer is also wrong. I read about how Joy and Dan had fun on a rainy day, so the third answer is the correct answer.*

PROMPT

You read about the great idea of making gum in "Gum" and about Joy and Dan's idea to have fun in "Rainy Day." Which idea do you think was <u>better</u>? Tell why.

Explain how to prepare for a constructed-response question: *In this part of the test, I have to write. I read the question to look for words that help me. There are titles from two stories, so I need to think about both stories. Here's an important word I can make a line under:* better. *What does it mean when something is better? So I need to pick one idea that I think is better and tell what makes it better.*

Model for children how to read the test itself. Proficient English readers may benefit from strategies such as reading the test question and answer options first and then skimming the selection to find information that will help them select the correct answer to the question. English language learners are not served well by this option. They need to read and understand the selection carefully and then consider how to answer the questions asked. Model this type of test-taking strategy for children as you think aloud and explain the process.

Summarize test formats and strategies for children. Consider making a T-chart to show examples of the question types that children may find on tests, such as fill-in-the-blank, matching, and multiple choice. If your T-chart is large enough to be a wall chart, include examples of each type of item from released tests and model tests on the chart. Explain what the structures are and what they ask test-takers to do (or ask children to explain as you teach various strategies).

Evaluation Chart: Grade 1 – Unit R Benchmark Test

Student Name _____ Date _____

Item	Tested Skill	Common Core State Standard	Score (circle one)
Reading – Parts 1–5			
Reading – Part 1: Phonemic Awareness			
1. [square]	Initial /m/	Foundational Skills 2.c	0 1
2. [circle]	Initial /y/	Foundational Skills 2.c	0 1
3. [triangle]	Initial /s/	Foundational Skills 2.c	0 1
4. [heart]	Final /p/	Foundational Skills 2.c	0 1
5. [square]	Final /t/	Foundational Skills 2.c	0 1
6. [circle]	Final /g/	Foundational Skills 2.c	0 1
7. [triangle]	Final /r/	Foundational Skills 2.c	0 1
8. [square]	Short *u* (CVC)	Foundational Skills 2.a.	0 1
9. [circle]	Short *i* (CVC)	Foundational Skills 2.a.	0 1
10. [triangle]	Short *e* (CVC)	Foundational Skills 2.a.	0 1
Reading – Part 2: Phonics			
11. [square]	Initial *p*	Foundational Skills 2.c.	0 1
12. [circle]	Initial *w*	Foundational Skills 2.c.	0 1
13. [triangle]	Initial *b*	Foundational Skills 2.c.	0 1
14. [heart]	Initial *qu*	Foundational Skills 2.c.	0 1
15. [rectangle]	Initial *j*	Foundational Skills 2.c.	0 1
16. [square]	Final *l*	Foundational Skills 2.c.	0 1
17. [circle]	Final *f*	Foundational Skills 2.c.	0 1
18. [triangle]	Final *r*	Foundational Skills 2.c.	0 1
19. [heart]	Final *x*	Foundational Skills 2.c.	0 1
20. [rectangle]	Final *d*	Foundational Skills 2.c.	0 1
Reading – Part 3: Word Reading			
21. [square]	CVC	Foundational Skills 3.c.	0 1
22. [circle]	CVC	Foundational Skills 3.c.	0 1
23. [triangle]	CVCC	Foundational Skills 3.c.	0 1
24. [heart]	CVC	Foundational Skills 3.c.	0 1
25. [rectangle]	CVC	Foundational Skills 3.c.	0 1
26. [square]	CVC	Foundational Skills 3.c.	0 1
27. [circle]	CVC	Foundational Skills 3.c.	0 1
28. [triangle]	CVCC	Foundational Skills 3.c.	0 1
29. [heart]	CVC	Foundational Skills 3.c.	0 1
30. [rectangle]	CVCC	Foundational Skills 3.c.	0 1

Evaluation Chart: Grade 1 – Unit R Benchmark Test

Reading – Part 4: Word Knowledge

31. [square]	High-frequency words	Foundational Skills 3.g.	0	1
32. [circle]	High-frequency words	Foundational Skills 3.g.	0	1
33. [triangle]	High-frequency words	Foundational Skills 3.g.	0	1
34. [heart]	High-frequency words	Foundational Skills 3.g.	0	1
35. [rectangle]	High-frequency words	Foundational Skills 3.g.	0	1
36. [square]	High-frequency words	Foundational Skills 3.g.	0	1
37. [circle]	High-frequency words	Foundational Skills 3.g.	0	1
38. [triangle]	High-frequency words	Foundational Skills 3.g.	0	1
39. [heart]	High-frequency words	Foundational Skills 3.g.	0	1
40. [rectangle]	High-frequency words	Foundational Skills 3.g.	0	1

Reading – Part 5: Comprehension

41. [square]	Literary elements: character	Literature 3.	0	1
42. [circle]	Literary elements: setting	Literature 3.	0	1
43. [triangle]	Realism/fantasy	Literature 5.	0	1
44. [heart]	Literary elements: plot	Literature 3.	0	1
45. [rectangle]	Realism/fantasy	Literature 5.	0	1
46. [square]	Literary elements: setting	Literature 3.	0	1
47. [triangle]	Main ideas and details	Literature 2.	0	1
48. [heart]	Literary elements: character	Literature 3.	0	1
49. [circle]	Literary elements: plot	Literature 3.	0	1
50. [rectangle]	Literary elements: plot	Literature 3.	0	1
Student's Reading Total Score/Total Possible Score _____ **/50**				

Reading percentage score: _____ ÷ 50 = _____ × 100 = _____%

(student's total score)   (percentage score)

Written Composition – Part 6	
Writing Score (Complete one.) _____/6 _____/5 _____/4 _____/3	**Common Core State Standards**
Notes/Observations:	Writing 3. Writing 5. Language 1. Language 2.

Evaluation Chart: Grade 1 – Unit 1 Benchmark Test

Student Name _____ Date _____

Item	Tested Skill	Item Type*	Common Core State Standard	Score (circle one)
Reading – Parts 1–4				
Reading – Part 1: Comprehension				
1.	Literary elements: character	L	Literature 7.	0 1
2.	Literary elements: setting	L	Literature 3.	0 1
3.	Realism/fantasy	I	Literature 5.	0 1
4.	Main idea	L	Literature 2.	0 1
5.	Setting	L	Literature 3.	0 1
6.	Genre (realism/fantasy)	I	Literature 3.	0 1
7.	Draw conclusions	I	Literature 2.	0 1
8.	Setting	L	Literature 1.	0 1
9.	Main idea	L	Literature 5.	0 1
10.	Main idea	I	Literature 2.	0 1
11.	Literary elements: character	I	Literature 3.	0 1
12.	Literary elements: character	I	Literature 3.	0 1
13.	Literary elements: character	I	Literature 3.	0 1
14.	Sequence	I	Literature 1.	0 1
Reading – Part 2: High-Frequency Words				
15.	High-frequency words		Foundational Skills 3.g.	0 1
16.	High-frequency words		Foundational Skills 3.g.	0 1
17.	High-frequency words		Foundational Skills 3.g.	0 1
18.	High-frequency words		Foundational Skills 3.g.	0 1
19.	High-frequency words		Foundational Skills 3.g.	0 1
20.	High-frequency words		Foundational Skills 3.g.	0 1
Reading – Part 3: Phonics				
21.	Short *a*		Foundational Skills 3.b.	0 1
22.	Short *o*/ck/ final consonant blend		Foundational Skills 3.b.	0 1
23.	Short *o*/x/		Foundational Skills 3.b.	0 1
24.	Short *e*		Foundational Skills 3.b.	0 1
25.	Short *o*		Foundational Skills 3.b.	0 1
26.	Plural *-s*		Foundational Skills 3.f.	0 1
27.	Inflected ending *-ing*		Foundational Skills 3.f.	0 1
28.	Short *i*		Foundational Skills 3.b.	0 1
29.	Initial consonant blend		Foundational Skills 3.b.	0 1
30.	Short *u*		Foundational Skills 3.b.	0 1

- -

Reading – Part 3: Phonics (continued)				
31.	Final consonant cluster	Foundational Skills 3.b.	0	1
32.	Inflected ending -s	Foundational Skills 3.f.	0	1
33.	Short e/ final consonant cluster	Foundational Skills 3.b.	0	1
34.	Short i	Foundational Skills 3.b.	0	1
Student's Regrouping Multiple-Choice Score/Total Possible Score _____ /34				
Reading – Part 4: Writing Conventions				
35.	Sentences	Language 1.	0	1
36.	Sentences	Language 1.c.	0	1
37.	Sentences	Language 1.c.	0	1
38.	Sentences	Language 1.	0	1
39.	Sentences	Language 2.b.	0	1
40.	Sentences	Language 2.b.	0	1
Student's Reading Total Score/Total Possible Score _____ /40				

*L = literal   I = inferential   C = critical analysis

Regrouping (Reading – Parts 1–3) percentage: _____ ÷ 34 = _____ × 100 = _____ %
                                                                     (student's score)   (percentage score)

Reading – Parts 1–4 percentage score: _____ ÷ 40 = _____ × 100 = _____ %
                                                              (student's total score)   (percentage score)

Writing – Part 5	Common Core State Standards
Writing Score (Complete one.) ____/6 ____/5 ____/4 ____/3	
Notes/Observations:	Writing 3. Writing 5. Language 1. Language 2.

Evaluation Chart: Grade 1 – Unit 2 Benchmark Test

Student Name _____ Date _____

Reading – Parts 1–4

Item	Tested Skill	Item Type*	Common Core State Standard	Score (circle one)
Reading – Part 1: Comprehension				
1.	Cause and effect	L	Literature 1.	0 1
2.	Main idea	I	Literature 2.	0 1
3.	Cause and effect	I	Literature 1.	0 1
4.	Sequence	L	Literature 1.	0 1
5.	Author's purpose	I	Literature 1.	0 1
6.	Main idea	I	Literature 2.	0 1
7.	Cause and effect	I	Literature 1.	0 1
8.	Main idea	I	Literature 2.	0 1
9.	Author's purpose	I	Literature 1.	0 1
10.	Genre (realism/fantasy)	I	Literature 5.	0 1
11.	Sequence	I	Literature 1.	0 1
12.	Author's purpose	I	Literature 1.	0 1
13.	Literary elements: setting	I	Literature 3.	0 1
14.	Literary elements: character	I	Literature 3.	0 1
Reading – Part 2: High-Frequency Words				
15.	High-frequency words		Foundational Skills 3.g.	0 1
16.	High-frequency words		Foundational Skills 3.g.	0 1
17.	High-frequency words		Foundational Skills 3.g.	0 1
18.	High-frequency words		Foundational Skills 3.g.	0 1
19.	High-frequency words		Foundational Skills 3.g.	0 1
20.	High-frequency words		Foundational Skills 3.g.	0 1
Reading – Part 3: Phonics				
21.	-*sh* Digraph		Foundational Skills 3.a.	0 1
22.	*a* sound in *ball;* -*ed* inflectional ending		Foundational Skills 3.b., 3.f.	0 1
23.	-*th* Digraph		Foundational Skills 3.a.	0 1
24.	Long *a* (CVCe)		Foundational Skills 3.c.	0 1
25.	Long *i* (CVCe)		Foundational Skills 3.c.	0 1
26.	*c*/s/		Foundational Skills 3.	0 1
27.	*ch* Digraph		Foundational Skills 3.a.	0 1
28.	*g*/j/		Foundational Skills 3.	0 1
29.	*tch* Digraph		Foundational Skills 3.a.	0 1
30.	Contraction '*ll*		Foundational Skills 3.	0 1

Reading – Part 3: Phonics (continued)

31.	*th* Digraph	Foundational Skills 3.a.	0 1
32.	Long *e*	Foundational Skills 3.c.	0 1
33.	Long *o* (CVCe)	Foundational Skills 3.c.	0 1
34.	Syllables VCCV	Foundational Skills 3.d.	0 1
Student's Regrouping Multiple-Choice Score/Total Possible Score			**/34**

Reading – Part 4: Writing Conventions

35.	Nouns	Language 1.b.	0 1
36.	Nouns	Language 1.b.	0 1
37.	Nouns	Language 2.a.	0 1
38.	Nouns	Language 2.a.	0 1
39.	Nouns	Language 2.a.	0 1
40.	Nouns	Language 2.a.	0 1
Student's Reading Total Score/Total Possible Score			**/40**

*L = literal   I = inferential   C = critical analysis

Regrouping (Reading – Parts 1–3) percentage: _____ ÷ 34 = _____ × 100 = _____%

(student's score)   (percentage score)

Reading – Parts 1–4 percentage score: _____ ÷ 40 = _____ × 100 = _____%

(student's total score)   (percentage score)

Writing – Part 5	Common Core State Standards
Writing Score (Complete one.) _____/6 _____/5 _____/4 _____/3	
Notes/Observations:	Writing 2. Writing 5. Language 1. Language 2.

Evaluation Chart: Grade 1 – Unit 3 Benchmark Test

Student Name _____ Date _____

Reading – Parts 1–4				
Item	**Tested Skill**	**Item Type***	**Common Core State Standard**	**Score** (circle one)
Reading – Part 1: Comprehension				
1.	Literary elements: plot	L	Literature 3.	0 1
2.	Compare/contrast	I	Literature 9.	0 1
3.	Compare/contrast	I	Literature 9.	0 1
4.	Sequence	L	Literature 1.	0 1
5.	Draw conclusions	I	Literature 1.	0 1
6.	Genre (realism/fantasy)	I	Literature 5.	0 1
7.	Author's purpose	I	Literature 1.	0 1
A.	Constructed-response text-to-self connection		Writing 1.	0 1 2
8.	Literary elements: plot	I	Literature 3.	0 1
9.	Sequence	L	Literature 1.	0 1
10.	Draw conclusions	I	Literature 1.	0 1
11.	Literary elements: theme	I	Literature 2.	0 1
12.	Sequence	L	Literature 1.	0 1
13.	Literary elements: plot	I	Literature 3.	0 1
14.	Compare/contrast	I	Literature 3.	0 1
B.	Constructed-response text-to-text connection		Literature 9.	0 1 2
Reading – Part 2: High-Frequency Words				
15.	High-frequency words		Foundational Skills 3.g.	0 1
16.	High-frequency words		Foundational Skills 3.g.	0 1
17.	High-frequency words		Foundational Skills 3.g.	0 1
18.	High-frequency words		Foundational Skills 3.g.	0 1
19.	High-frequency words		Foundational Skills 3.g.	0 1
20.	High-frequency words		Foundational Skills 3.g.	0 1
Reading – Part 3: Phonics				
21.	Long *i* vowel sound of *y*		Foundational Skills 3.c.	0 1
22.	Long *e* vowel sound of *y*		Foundational Skills 3.c.	0 1
23.	Long vowel pattern CV		Foundational Skills 3.c.	0 1
24.	Compound word		Foundational Skills 3.	0 1
25.	Word family *ng*		Foundational Skills 3.	0 1
26.	Long vowel pattern CV		Foundational Skills 3.c.	0 1
27.	*-es* Plural		Foundational Skills 3.f.	0 1
28.	Word family *nk*		Foundational Skills 3.	0 1

Reading – Part 3: Phonics (continued)				
29.	r-Controlled *ore*	Foundational Skills 3.	0	1
30.	Contraction *'s*	Foundational Skills 3.	0	1
31.	Comparative *-est*	Foundational Skills 3.	0	1
32.	r-Controlled *ar*	Foundational Skills 3.	0	1
33.	Inflected ending *-ed* with double final consonant	Foundational Skills 3.f.	0	1
34.	Contraction *'ve*	Foundational Skills 3.	0	1
Student's Regrouping Multiple-Choice Score/Total Possible Score _____ /34				

Reading – Part 4: Writing Conventions				
35.	Verbs	Language 1.	0	1
36.	Verbs	Language 1.c.	0	1
37.	Verbs	Language 1.c.	0	1
38.	Verbs	Language 1.e.	0	1
39.	Verbs	Language 1.e.	0	1
40.	Verbs	Language 2.	0	1
Student's Reading Total Score/Total Possible Score _____ /44				

*L = literal   I = inferential   C = critical analysis

Regrouping (Reading – Parts 1–3) percentage: _____ ÷ 34 = _____ × 100 = _____%
(student's score)   (percentage score)

Reading – Parts 1–4 percentage score: _____ ÷ 44 = _____ × 100 = _____%
(student's total score)   (percentage score)

Writing – Part 5	Common Core State Standards
Writing Score (Complete one.) _____/6 _____/5 _____/4 _____/3	
Notes/Observations:	Writing 2. Writing 5. Language 1. Language 2.

Evaluation Chart: Grade 1 – Unit 4 Benchmark Test

Student Name _____ Date _____

Item	**Tested Skill**	**Item Type***	**Common Core State Standard**	**Score** (circle one)
Reading – Part 1: Comprehension				
1.	Cause and effect	L	Literature 1.	0 1
2.	Author's purpose	I	Literature 1.	0 1
3.	Draw conclusions	I	Literature 1.	0 1
4.	Draw conclusions	I	Literature 1.	0 1
5.	Literary elements: theme	I	Literature 2.	0 1
6.	Draw conclusions	I	Literature 1.	0 1
7.	Literary elements: plot	I	Literature 3.	0 1
A.	Constructed-response text-to-self connection		Writing 3.	0 1 2
8.	Sequence	L	Informational Text 1.	0 1
9.	Main idea	I	Informational Text 2.	0 1
10.	Fact and opinion	I	Informational Text 1.	0 1
11.	Author's purpose	I	Informational Text 8.	0 1
12.	Cause and effect	L	Informational Text 1.	0 1
13.	Cause and effect	L	Informational Text 1.	0 1
14.	Fact and opinion	I	Informational Text 1.	0 1
B.	Constructed-response text-to-text connection		Literature 9.	0 1 2
Reading – Part 2: High-Frequency Words				
15.	High-frequency words		Foundational Skills 3.g.	0 1
16.	High-frequency words		Foundational Skills 3.g.	0 1
17.	High-frequency words		Foundational Skills 3.g.	0 1
18.	High-frequency words		Foundational Skills 3.g.	0 1
19.	High-frequency words		Foundational Skills 3.g.	0 1
20.	High-frequency words		Foundational Skills 3.g.	0 1
Reading – Part 3: Phonics				
21.	Long *a: ay*		Foundational Skills 3.c.	0 1
22.	Long *o: ow, oa*		Foundational Skills 3.c.	0 1
23.	Long *e: ea*		Foundational Skills 3.c.	0 1
24.	Long *i: igh*		Foundational Skills 3.c.	0 1
25.	Vowels *oo, ui*		Foundational Skills 3.c.	0 1
26.	Consonant sound *wr*/r/		Foundational Skills 3.c.	0 1
27.	Possessives		Foundational Skills 3.	0 1
28.	Suffix *-ful*		Foundational Skills 3.	0 1

Reading – Part 3: Phonics (continued)

29.	Vowels *ew, ue*	Foundational Skills 3.c.	0	1
30.	Consonant sound *kn*/n/	Foundational Skills 3.	0	1
31.	Compound words	Foundational Skills 3.	0	1
32.	Short *e: ea*	Foundational Skills 3.	0	1
33.	Long *a: ai*	Foundational Skills 3.c.	0	1
34.	Suffix *-ly*	Foundational Skills 3.	0	1

Student's Regrouping Multiple-Choice Score/Total Possible Score _____ **/34**

Reading – Part 4: Writing Conventions

35.	Adjectives	Language 1.f.	0	1
36.	Adjectives	Language 1.f.	0	1
37.	Adjectives	Language 1.f.	0	1
38.	Adjectives	Language 1.f.	0	1
39.	Adjectives	Language 1.f.	0	1
40.	Adjectives	Language 1.f.	0	1

Student's Reading Total Score/Total Possible Score _____ **/44**

*L = literal   I = inferential   C = critical analysis

Regrouping (Reading – Parts 1–3) percentage: _____ ÷ 34 = _____ × 100 = _____ %
                              (student's score)   (percentage score)

Reading – Parts 1–4 percentage score: _____ ÷ 44 = _____ × 100 = _____ %
                            (student's total score)   (percentage score)

Writing – Part 5

	Common Core State Standards
Writing Score (Complete one.) _____/6 _____/5 _____/4 _____/3	
Notes/Observations:	Writing 1. Writing 5. Language 1. Language 2.

Evaluation Chart: Grade 1 – Unit 5 Benchmark Test

Student Name _____ Date _____

Item	Tested Skill	Item Type*	Common Core State Standards	Score (circle one)
Reading – Part 1: Comprehension				
1.	Literary elements: setting	L	Literature 3.	0 1
2.	Literary elements: theme	I	Literature 2.	0 1
3.	Cause and effect	L	Literature 1.	0 1
4.	Literary elements: theme	I	Literature 2.	0 1
5.	Literary elements: plot	I	Literature 3.	0 1
6.	Main idea	I	Literature 2.	0 1
7.	Literary elements: character	I	Literature 3.	0 1
A.	Constructed-response text-to-self connection		Writing 3.	0 1 2
8.	Facts and details	L	Informational Text 1.	0 1
9.	Compare/contrast	I	Informational Text 3.	0 1
10.	Author's purpose	I	Informational Text 8.	0 1
11.	Facts and details	L	Informational Text 1.	0 1
12.	Main idea	I	Informational Text 2.	0 1
13.	Facts and details	I	Informational Text 1.	0 1
14.	Draw conclusions	I	Informational Text 1.	0 1
B.	Constructed-response text-to-text connection		Writing 1.	0 1 2
Reading – Part 2: High-Frequency Words				
15.	High-frequency words		Foundational Skills 3.g.	0 1
16.	High-frequency words		Foundational Skills 3.g.	0 1
17.	High-frequency words		Foundational Skills 3.g.	0 1
18.	High-frequency words		Foundational Skills 3.g.	0 1
19.	High-frequency words		Foundational Skills 3.g.	0 1
20.	High-frequency words		Foundational Skills 3.g.	0 1
Reading – Part 3: Phonics				
21.	Syllables V/CV		Foundational Skills 3.e.	0 1
22.	Vowel diphthong *ou*		Foundational Skills 3.	0 1
23.	Prefix *un-*		Language 4.b.	0 1
24.	Vowel diphthong *oy*		Foundational Skills 3.	0 1
25.	Vowel diphthong *aw*		Foundational Skills 3.	0 1
26.	Inflected ending *-ed* (drop *e* before *-ed*)		Foundational Skills 3.f.	0 1
27.	Inflected ending *-ing* (drop *e* before *-ing*)		Foundational Skills 3.f.	0 1
28.	Long vowel pattern *i (nd)*		Foundational Skills 3.	0 1

Reading – Part 3: Phonics (continued)

29.	Suffix *-er* (agent)	Language 4.b.	0	1
30.	Compound words	Foundational Skills 3.	0	1
31.	Vowel diphthong *-ow*	Foundational Skills 3.	0	1
32.	Final syllable *-le*	Foundational Skills 3.c.	0	1
33.	Long vowel pattern *o* (*st*)	Foundational Skills 3.c.	0	1
34.	Vowels: *oo* as in *foot*	Foundational Skills 3.c.	0	1
Student's Regrouping Multiple-Choice Score/Total Possible Score			**_____/34**	

Reading – Part 4: Writing Conventions

35.	Pronouns	Language 1.d.	0	1
36.	Pronouns	Language 1.d.	0	1
37.	Adverbs	Language 1.	0	1
38.	Pronouns	Language 1.d.	0	1
39.	Pronouns	Language 1.d.	0	1
40.	Sentences	Language 1.	0	1
Student's Reading Total Score/Total Possible Score			**_____/44**	

*L = literal   I = inferential   C = critical analysis

Regrouping (Reading – Parts 1–3) percentage: _____ ÷ 34 = _____ × 100 = _____%

(student's score)   (percentage score)

Reading – Parts 1–4 percentage score: _____ ÷ 44 = _____ × 100 = _____%

(student's total score)   (percentage score)

Writing – Part 5	Common Core State Standards
Writing Score (Complete one.) _____/6 _____/5 _____/4 _____/3	
Notes/Observations:	Writing 3. Writing 5. Language 1. Language 2.

Evaluation Chart: Grade 1 – End-of-Year Benchmark Test

Student Name _____ Date _____

	Reading – Parts 1–4			
Item	Tested Skill	Item Type*	Common Core State Standard	Score (circle one)
1.	Literary elements: setting	I	Literature 3.	0 1
2.	Draw conclusions	I	Literature 1.	0 1
3.	Realism/fantasy	I	Literature 5.	0 1
4.	Main idea (fiction)	I	Literature 2.	0 1
5.	Facts and details	I	Literature 1.	0 1
6.	Literary elements: character	I	Literature 3.	0 1
7.	Literary elements: plot	L	Literature 3.	0 1
8.	Sequence	L	Literature 1.	0 1
9.	Literary elements: character	I	Literature 3.	0 1
10.	Draw conclusions	I	Literature 1.	0 1
11.	Main idea (fiction)	I	Literature 2.	0 1
12.	Author's purpose	I	Literature 1.	0 1
13.	Facts and details	L	Literature 1.	0 1
14.	Literary elements: theme	I	Literature 2.	0 1
A.	Contructed-response item – text-to-text connection		Writing 2.	0 1 2
15.	Fact and opinion	I	Informational Text 1.	0 1
16.	Sequence	I	Informational Text 3.	0 1
17.	Compare/contrast	I	Informational Text 3.	0 1
18.	Cause and effect	I	Informational Text 3.	0 1
19.	Compare/contrast	I	Informational Text 3.	0 1
20.	Sequence	L	Informational Text 3.	0 1
21.	Author's purpose	I	Informational Text 8.	0 1
B.	Constructed-response item – text-to-text connection		Writing 1.	0 1 2
22.	High-frequency words		Foundational Skills 3.g.	0 1
23.	High-frequency words		Foundational Skills 3.g.	0 1
24.	High-frequency words		Foundational Skills 3.g.	0 1
25.	High-frequency words		Foundational Skills 3.g.	0 1
26.	High-frequency words		Foundational Skills 3.g.	0 1
27.	High-frequency words		Foundational Skills 3.g.	0 1
28.	High-frequency words		Foundational Skills 3.g.	0 1
29.	High-frequency words		Foundational Skills 3.g.	0 1
30.	High-frequency words		Foundational Skills 3.g.	0 1
31.	Vowel diphthong *oy, oi*/oi/		Foundational Skills 3.	0 1
32.	Inflected ending *-ing*		Foundational Skills 3.f.	0 1
33.	Long *a*: CVCe; *c*/s/		Foundational Skills 3.c.	0 1
34.	Contraction *n't*		Foundational Skills 3.	0 1
35.	Long *e: ea, ee*		Foundational Skills 3.c.	0 1

Reading – Parts 1–4 (continued)

36.	Syllables V/CV	Foundational Skills 3.e.	0	1
37.	Compound words	Foundational Skills 3.	0	1
38.	Vowel pattern *ew, ue*	Foundational Skills 3.	0	1
39.	Comparative ending *-est*	Language 4.b.	0	1
40.	Vowels *oo* as in *moon*	Foundational Skills 3.	0	1
41.	Vowel diphthong *ow, ou*/ou/	Foundational Skills 3.	0	1
42.	Long *a: ai, ay*	Foundational Skills 3.c.	0	1
43.	Suffix *-ful*	Language 4.b.	0	1
44.	Consonant sound *kn*/n/	Foundational Skills 3.	0	1
45.	Long *i: igh*	Foundational Skills 3.	0	1
46.	Long *o: ow*	Foundational Skills 3.	0	1
47.	Suffix *-er* (agent)	Language 4.b.	0	1
48.	Short *e: ea*	Foundational Skills 3.	0	1
49.	Comparative ending *-er*	Language 4.b.	0	1
50.	Vowels *oo* as in *book*	Foundational Skills 3.	0	1
51.	Long vowel pattern *o (ld)*	Foundational Skills 3.	0	1
52.	Sentences	Language 1.	0	1
53.	Nouns	Language 1.b.	0	1
54.	Verbs	Language 1.e.	0	1
55.	Adjectives	Language 1.f.	0	1
56.	Pronouns	Language 1.d.	0	1
57.	Verbs	Language 1.e.	0	1
58.	Pronouns	Language 1.d.	0	1
59.	Nouns	Language 1.b.	0	1
60.	Verbs	Language 1.	0	1

Student's Reading Total Score/Total Possible Score _____**/64**

*L = literal   I = inferential   C = critical analysis

Reading – Parts 1–4 percentage score: _____ ÷ 64 = _____ × 100 = _____%
         (student's total score)   (percentage score)

Writing – Part 5

Writing Score (Complete one.) _____/6 _____/5 _____/4 _____/3	Common Core State Standards
Notes/Observations:	Writing 3. Writing 5. Language 1. Language 2.

CLASS RECORD CHART

Grade 1 Unit Benchmark Tests

Teacher Name _____   Class _____

Student Name	Unit R		Unit 1		Unit 2		Unit 3		Unit 4		Unit 5	
	Pt 1–5	Pt 6	Pt 1–4	Pt 5	Pt 1–4	Pt 5	Pt 1–4	Pt 5	Pt 1–4	Pt 5	Pt 1–4	Pt 5
1.												
2.												
3.												
4.												
5.												
6.												
7.												
8.												
9.												
10.												
11.												
12.												
13.												
14.												
15.												
16.												
17.												
18.												
19.												
20.												
21.												
22.												
23.												
24.												
25.												
26.												
27.												
28.												
29.												
30.												

- - - CLASS RECORD CHART -

DIRECTIONS – UNIT R TEST

READING – PART 1: PHONEMIC AWARENESS
(Individual or small group)

Purpose: Assesses ability to recognize initial sounds and final sounds and to blend individual phonemes.

Hand out student test booklets. Have children turn to page 2. Use the first set of directions to administer the first 8 questions of the test, beginning with the sample question. When you reach question 9, read the second set of directions. Directions in **bold** are to be read aloud. The others are for your information only.

We are going to listen for sounds in words. Find the small star. Put your finger on it. Now look at the three pictures in the row beside the star: *wave, mouse, watch*. Listen to the beginning sound of each word: *wave, mouse, watch*. Two of the words begin with the same sound. One of the words begins with a different sound. Which two words have the same beginning sound? (Pause). **Yes, *wave* and *watch* have the same beginning sound. Draw a circle around the pictures of the *wave* and the *watch*.**

When you are sure that each child understands the task and has followed the directions for completing the sample item, administer each test item.

1. **Move down to the next row where you see the square. Put your finger on the square. Now look at the three pictures in the same row: *nut, mug, mask*. Draw a circle around the two pictures that have the same sound at the beginning: *nut . . . mug . . . mask*.**

2. **Move down to the next row where you see the circle. Put your finger on the circle. Now look at the three pictures in the same row: *yak, yolk, worm*. Draw a circle around the two pictures that have the same sound at the beginning: *yak . . . yolk . . . worm*.**

3. **Move down to the next row where you see the triangle. Put your finger on the triangle. Now look at the three pictures in the same row: *sun, house, seal*. Draw a circle around the two pictures that have the same sound at the beginning: *sun . . . house . . . seal*.**

4. **Move down to the next row where you see the heart. Put your finger on the heart. Listen for the ending sound: *ring, map, top*. Draw a circle around the two pictures that have the same sound at the end: *ring . . . map . . . top*.**

5. **Go to the top of the next page. Look at the top row where you see the square. Put your finger on the square. Look at the three pictures. Listen for the ending sound: *bat, kite, rug*. Draw a circle around the two pictures that have the same sound at the end: *bat . . . kite . . . rug*.**

6. **Move down to the next row where you see the circle. Put your finger on the circle. Look at the three pictures. Listen for the ending sound:** *dog, cat, pig.* **Draw a circle around the two pictures that have the same sound at the end:** *dog . . . cat . . . pig.*

7. **Move down to the next row where you see the triangle. Put your finger on the triangle. Look at the three pictures. Listen for the ending sound:** *soap, bear, door.* **Draw a circle around the two pictures that have the same sound at the end:** *soap . . . bear . . . door.*

Go to the top of the next page. Now we are going to do something a little bit different. We are going to listen to all of the sounds in a word. Look at the top row where you see the star. Put your finger on the star. Now look at the three pictures in that row. I am going to say a word. Listen to the sounds I say: */b/ /e/ /d/.* **Blend the sounds together. What word is it?** (Pause) **Yes, the word is** *bed.* **Which picture goes with the word** */b/ /e/ /d/?* **Yes, the first picture is a** */b/ /e/ /d/ . . . bed.* **Draw a circle around the first picture of the bed.**

When you are sure that each child understands the task and has followed the directions for completing the sample item, administer each test item.

8. **Move down to the next row where you see the square. Put your finger on the square. Look at the three pictures in that row. Which picture is a** */b/ /u/ /s/?* **Circle the picture of the** */b/ /u/ /s/.*

9. **Move down to the next row where you see the circle. Put your finger on the circle. Look at the three pictures in that row. Which picture is a** */f/ /i/ /n/?* **Circle the picture of the** */f/ /i/ /n/.*

10. **Move down to the next row where you see the triangle. Put your finger on it. Look at the three pictures in that row. Which picture is a** */j/ /e/ /t/?* **Circle the picture of the** */j/ /e/ /t/.*

When children have finished the last question, point out the stop sign at the bottom of the page. Explain that this sign means that the children should stop what they are doing. They should not go on to the next page until they are told to do so. At this point, you may want to take a break. When the children are ready, proceed with Part 2.

READING – PART 2: PHONICS
(Individual or small group)

Purpose: Assesses ability to connect sound to letter.

Hand out student pages 5–6. Use the following directions to administer the assessment, beginning with the sample question.

Now we are going to match a letter to its sound. Let's do the first one together. Find the small star. Put your finger on it. Now look at the letter by the star. It is the letter v. What is the sound of the letter v? (Have a child give the sound of the letter *v*.) **Now look at the three pictures in the same row: *van, pants, goat*. Which word begins with the sound of the letter v?** (Pause) **Yes, *van* begins with the sound of the letter v. Draw a circle around the picture of the *van* because *van* begins with the letter v.**

When you are sure that each child understands the task and has followed the directions for completing the sample item, administer each test item.

11. **Move down to the next row where you see the square. Put your finger on the square. Look at the *p*. Look at the pictures: *bear, pot, heart*. Circle the picture that begins with the sound of the letter *p*.**

12. **Move down to the next row where you see the circle. Put your finger on the circle. Look at the *w*. Look at the pictures: *nest, lamb, web*. Circle the picture that begins with the sound of the letter *w*.**

13. **Move down to the next row where you see the triangle. Put your finger on the triangle. Look at the *b*. Look at the pictures: *tent, bowl, horse*. Circle the picture that begins with the sound of the letter *b*.**

14. **Move down to the next row where you see the heart. Put your finger on the heart. Look at the *qu*. Look at the pictures: *quilt, doll, hat*. Circle the picture that begins with the sound of the letters *qu*.**

15. **Move down to the next row where you see the rectangle. Put your finger on the rectangle. Look at the *j*. Look at the pictures: *fence, hive, jet*. Circle the picture that begins with the sound of the letter *j*.**

16. **Go to the next page. Look at the top row where you see the square. Put your finger on the square. Look at the *l*. Look at the pictures. Listen for the ending sound: *shell, can, broom*. Circle the picture that ends with the sound of the letter *l*.**

17. **Move down to the next row where you see the circle. Put your finger on the circle. Look at the *f*. Look at the pictures. Listen for the ending sound: *wheel, snake, roof*. Circle the picture that ends with the sound of the letter *f*.**

18. **Move down to the next row where you see the triangle. Put your finger on the triangle. Look at the *r*. Look at the pictures. Listen for the ending sound: *bear, foot, leaf*. Circle the picture that ends with the sound of the letter *r*.**

■ ■

19. Move down to the next row where you see the heart. Put your finger on the heart. Look at the *x*. Look at the pictures. Listen for the ending sound: *coat, box, egg.* Circle the picture that ends with the sound of the letter *x*.

20. Move down to the next row where you see the rectangle. Put your finger on the rectangle. Look at the *d*. Look at the pictures. Listen for the ending sound: *bed, map, fan.* Circle the picture that ends with the sound of the letter *d*.

When children have finished the last question, point out the stop sign at the bottom of the page. Explain that this sign means that the children should stop what they are doing. They should not go on to the next page until they are told to do so. At this point, you may want to take a break. When children are ready, proceed with Part 3.

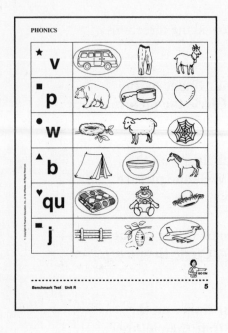

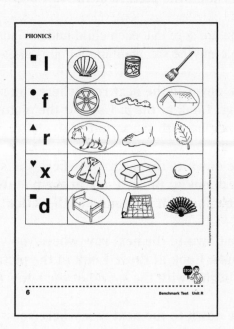

READING – PART 3: WORD READING
(Individual or small group)

Purpose: Assesses ability to read CVC and CVCC words.

Hand out student pages 7–8. Use the following directions to administer the assessment, beginning with the sample question.

Now we are going to find some words you know. Let's do the first one together. Find the small star. Put your finger on it. Now look at the picture by the star. It is a *hat*. Look at the three words in the same row. Which word spells *hat*? (Pause.) **Yes, the first word in the row is *hat*. *Hat* is spelled *h, a, t*. Draw a circle around the word *hat*.**

When you are sure that each child understands the task and has followed the directions for completing the sample item, administer each test item.

21. **Move down to the next row where you see the square. Put your finger on the square. Look at the picture. It is a *bus*. Look at the words in the row. Circle the word *bus*.**

22. **Move down to the next row where you see the circle. Put your finger on the circle. Look at the picture. It is a *leg*. Look at the words in the row. Circle the word *leg*.**

23. **Move down to the next row where you see the triangle. Put your finger on the triangle. Look at the picture. It is a *desk*. Look at the words in the row. Circle the word *desk*.**

24. **Move down to the next row where you see the heart. Put your finger on the heart. Look at the picture. It is a *pen*. Look at the words in the row. Circle the word *pen*.**

25. **Move down to the next row where you see a rectangle. Put your finger on the rectangle. Look at the picture. It is a *net*. Look at the words in the row. Circle the word *net*.**

26. **Go to the next page. Look at the top row where you see the square. Put your finger on the square. Look at the picture. It is a *mop*. Look at the words in the row. Circle the word *mop*.**

27. **Move down to the next row where you see the circle. Put your finger on the circle. Look at the picture. It is a *cup*. Look at the words in the row. Circle the word *cup*.**

28. **Move down to the next row where you see the triangle. Put your finger on the triangle. Look at the picture. It is a *lamp*. Look at the words in the row. Circle the word *lamp*.**

29. **Move down to the next row where you see the heart. Put your finger on the heart. Look at the picture. It is a *web*. Look at the words in the row. Circle the word *web*.**

30. Move down to the next row where you see a rectangle. Put your finger on the rectangle. Look at the picture. It is a *gift*. Look at the words in the row. Circle the word *gift*.

When children have finished the last question, point out the stop sign at the bottom of the page. Explain that this sign means that the children should stop what they are doing. They should not go on to the next page until they are told to do so. At this point, you may want to take a break. When children are ready, proceed with Part 4.

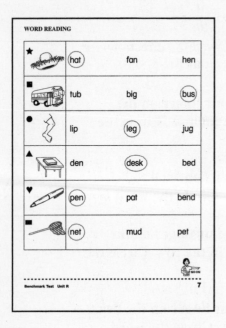

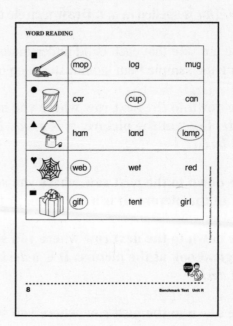

READING – PART 4: WORD KNOWLEDGE – HIGH-FREQUENCY WORDS

(Individual or small group)

Purpose: Assesses ability to immediately recognize high-frequency words.

Hand out student pages 9–10. Children are to circle each word as you say it aloud. Move through the assessment quickly to make sure you are assessing the child's ability to recognize the high-frequency word quickly.

31. **I am going to say one word in each row. You are going to circle the word I say. Find the first row with the square in it. Put your finger on it. Now look at the three words in that row. Draw a circle around the word** *the . . . the.*

32. **Move down to the next row. Put your finger on the circle. Look at the three words. Circle the word** *yellow . . . yellow.*

33. **Move down to the next row. Put your finger on the triangle. Look at the three words. Circle the word** *is . . . is.*

34. **Move down to the next row. Put your finger on the heart. Look at the three words. Circle the word** *like . . . like.*

35. **Move down to the next row. Put your finger on the rectangle. Look at the three words. Circle the word** *here . . . here.*

36. **Go to the next page. Look at the top row with the square in it. Put your finger on the square. Look at the three words. Circle the word** *look . . . look.*

37. **Move down to the next row. Put your finger on the circle. Look at the three words. Circle the word** *they . . . they.*

38. **Move down to the next row. Put your finger on the triangle. Look at the three words. Circle the word** *for . . . for.*

39. **Move down to the next row. Put your finger on the heart. Look at the three words. Circle the word** *you . . . you.*

40. **Move down to the next row. Put your finger on the rectangle. Look at the three words. Circle the word** *three . . . three.*

When children have finished the last question, point out the stop sign at the bottom of the page. Explain that this sign means that the children should stop what they are doing. They should not go on to the next page until they are told to do so. At this point, you may want to take a break. When children are ready, proceed with Part 5.

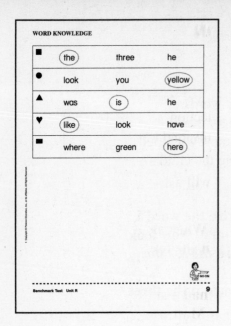

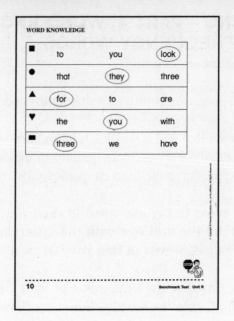

Benchmark Tests Teacher's Manual

READING – PART 5: LISTENING COMPREHENSION

(Individual, small group, or whole class)

Purpose: Assesses general comprehension.

Hand out student pages 11–12. Read aloud the introduction and the selection printed in **bold.** Then read each question that follows. Children are to respond by circling the best answer to each question.

I am going to read a selection about a kitten named Katie. Then I will ask you some questions. Listen carefully. Here is the selection.

Katie the kitten lived in a big house. She was very happy there. When she was sleepy, she loved to lie in the sunshine in the living room. When she felt playful she would find a toy and play.

There was only one thing Katie did not like about her house. It had a small mouse living in it. The mouse was named Matt. Katie thought that Matt was a bother. Matt always wanted to play with Katie. But Katie thought that a mouse wouldn't be a good playmate. He was too small. Whenever Matt asked Katie if she wanted to play, Katie said, "Why don't you go and play with someone your own size?"

One day Katie noticed an open window in the living room. She jumped up onto the window and sniffed the air. It smelled wonderful. Katie jumped out of the window into the backyard.

She had a wonderful time exploring the backyard. But when Katie was tired she wanted to go back inside. She walked to the window and tried to jump back into the house. But the window was too high. Katie felt very sad and began to cry. She heard a little voice say, "I know another way to get into the house."

Katie looked over and saw Matt.

"Follow me," said Matt. Katie followed Matt to the back door. Matt squeezed through a hole in the screen door and Katie went in after him. When she was inside she thought about how she hadn't been very nice to Matt. Now she understood that even if Matt was small, he could still be her friend.

"Hey Matt," Katie said. "Do you want to play?"

"Sure!" said Matt with a smile.

Now I am going to ask you some questions about the selection. For each question there are three pictures. Draw a circle around the picture that shows the best answer. Listen carefully.

41. Look at the first row of pictures at the top of the page where there is a square. Put your finger on the square. What kind of animal was Katie? Circle the picture that shows what kind of animal Katie was.

42. Move down to the next row of pictures where you see the circle. Put your finger on the circle. Where did Katie live? Circle the picture that shows where Katie lived.

43. Move down to the next row where you see the triangle. Put your finger on the triangle. How can you tell this selection is make-believe? Circle the picture that shows how you can tell this selection is make-believe.

44. Move down to the next row where you see the heart. Put your finger on the heart. What did Katie do when she couldn't jump into the house through the window? Circle the picture that shows what Katie did when she couldn't jump into the house through the window.

45. Move down to the next row where you see the rectangle. Put your finger on the rectangle. What part of this selection could really happen? Circle the picture that shows the part of this selection that could really happen.

When children have finished the last item, have them go to page 12 and look at the first row of pictures.

Now I am going to read another selection. This selection is about a boy named Daryl. After I read the selection I will ask you some questions. Listen carefully. Here is the selection.

Daryl was taking a walk with his mom. They were in the forest behind their house. Daryl loved being in the forest. Every time he and his mom came here, they found something new and interesting.

It was a spring day. The sun was shining and the air was warm. Daryl saw that some trees had buds on their branches. Other trees were covered with beautiful flowers. The air smelled fresh.

Daryl looked at the ground as he walked through the woods. He thought that he saw something blue on the ground next to a tree. He stopped walking. When Daryl bent down to get a better look, he found a small blue egg.

Daryl felt worried. He did not want the egg to be on the ground. Daryl carefully picked up the egg. He began looking for a bird's nest.

After a few minutes he found the nest. It was on a low branch in the tree. Daryl saw a mother bird sitting on the nest. He carefully put the egg back in the nest with the mother bird. He watched the mother bird for a few minutes and felt happy that he could help her.

Then Daryl and his mother began walking again. They wanted to see what else they could find.

Now I am going to ask you some questions about the selection. For each question there are three pictures. Draw a circle around the picture that shows the best answer. Listen carefully.

46. Look at the first row of pictures at the top of the page where there is a square. Put your finger on the square. Where did Daryl and his mom go for a walk? Circle the picture that shows where Daryl and his mom went for a walk.

47. Move down to the next row of pictures where you see the triangle. Put your finger on the triangle. What did Daryl find on the ground under the tree? Circle the picture that shows what Daryl found on the ground under the tree.

48. Move down to the next row where you see the heart. Put your finger on the heart. How did Daryl feel when he found the egg—surprised, worried, or happy? Circle the picture that shows how Daryl felt when he found the egg.

49. Move down to the next row where you see the circle. Put your finger on the circle. What did Daryl do after he found the egg on the ground? Circle the picture that shows what Daryl did.

50. Move down to the next row where you see the rectangle. Put your finger on the rectangle. What did Daryl see when he looked in the bird's nest? Circle the picture that shows what Daryl saw when he looked in the bird's nest.

When children have finished the last question, point out the stop sign at the bottom of the page. Explain that this sign means that the children should stop what they are doing. They should not go on to the next page until they are told to do so. At this point, you may want to take a break. When children are ready, proceed with Part 6.

WRITING — PART 6

(Individual, small group, or whole class)

Purpose: Assesses ability to write using nouns and pronouns.

Hand out student page 13. Read the prompt aloud. Then read through the checklist for writers. Point out the lines on page 13 and make sure the children know that they should write their responses on these lines. You may wish to give children scrap paper to use to plan their writing. Instruct children as follows.

Now we will be doing something different. You are going to draw a picture and write about your picture. Remember that a noun is the name of a person, animal, place, or thing. A pronoun is a word that takes the place of a noun. Draw a picture. Then write two sentences that use nouns and pronouns to tell about your picture.

Note: If children have trouble thinking of something to draw, remind them of some of the things they have learned about.

Here are some things to remember when you are drawing and writing:

Checklist:

Plan your picture and sentences before you begin drawing and writing.

Check that your picture shows a person, animal, place, or thing.

Check that your sentences contain a noun and pronoun that tell about your picture.

Begin your sentences with capital letters.

End your sentences with end marks.

Make sure your sentences make sense.

Make sure the words are spelled correctly. If you are not sure how to spell a word, sound out the word and spell it as best you can.

Make sure your sentences are the way you want readers to read it.

Now draw a picture of a person, animal, place, or thing. Then write two sentences about it that use nouns and pronouns to tell about it.

Give children fifteen to twenty minutes to complete their activity.

SCORING WRITING – PART 6

Prompt: Children are asked to draw a picture of a person, animal, place, or thing and write two sentences that use at least one noun and one pronoun to tell about the picture.

Scoring: Assess children's drawing based on how well the drawing addresses the suggested task and its level of detail. Assess children's writing based on how well it relates to the drawing and its use of nouns and pronouns. Use one of the Descriptive Writing Scoring Rubrics on pages T13–T14 to help you assess children's compositions. Assign each composition a score based on the 6-point, 5-point, 4-point, or 3-point scale.

DIRECTIONS – UNIT TEST 1

This is a test about reading and writing. In the first part, we will read a story and answer some questions about it.

READING – PART 1: COMPREHENSION

Selection: "Ox and Bird"

Directions in **bold** are to be read aloud; others are for your information only.

Read the directions on page 2.

Directions: Read about how Ox tries to help Bird. Then answer Numbers 1 through 14.

Now we are going to read the story "Ox and Bird." I will read the story aloud. Follow along on your test pages as I read. When I have finished, I will ask you some questions about the story. Listen carefully.

When children are ready, read aloud the story on pages 2 through 5 of the test pages. Pause to allow time for them to look at the picture on each page. Check to make sure that the children follow along and are on the right page. When you have finished reading the story, have children turn to page 6.

Questions 1–14

Now turn to page 6. I am going to ask you some questions about the story. Draw a circle around the best answer to each question. Listen carefully.

Make sure children are on page 6. Read each question number and the question aloud. Pause after each question to allow children to mark their answers.

1. **Look at the three pictures in the top row. Which picture shows what Ox was doing in the story? Draw a circle around what Ox was doing in this story.**

2. **Move down to the next row. Look at the pictures. Where was Bird in this story? Draw a circle around the picture that shows where Bird was.**

3. **Move down to the next row. Look at the pictures. What part of this story could really happen? Draw a circle around the picture that shows the part of the story that could really happen.**

4. **Move down to the next row. Why couldn't Bird play? Draw a circle around the sentence that explains why Bird couldn't play.**

Have children go on to the next page.

5. **Look at the pictures in the first row at the top of the page. What was the weather like in this story? Draw a circle around the picture that shows what the weather was like in this story.**

6. **Move down to the next row. How can you tell that this story is make-believe? Draw a circle around the sentence that explains why the story is make-believe.**

7. **Move down to the next row. Look at the pictures. Why did Bird have to stay in the tree? Draw a circle around the picture that shows why Bird had to stay in the tree.**

8. **Move down to the next row. Find the words that finish this sentence correctly. In this story Ox was *where?* Draw a circle around the words that tell where Ox was.**

Point out the Go On symbol and have children go on to the next page.

9. **Look at the sentences at the top of the page. Why can't Ox go up into the tree? Draw a circle around the sentence that explains why Ox can't go up into the tree.**

10. **Move down to the next row. What would be a good name for this story? Draw a circle around the name you think would be a good name for this story.**

11. **Move down to the next row. What did Ox want to do? Draw a circle around the words that answer what Ox wanted to do.**

12. **Move down to the next row. Look at the pictures. How did Bird feel at the end of the story? Draw a circle around the picture that shows how Bird felt at the end of the story.**

Have children go on to the next page.

13. **Look at the pictures in the first row at the top of the page. How did Ox feel at the end of the story? Draw a circle around the picture that shows how Ox felt at the end of the story.**

14. **Move down to the next row. What happened last in the story? Draw a circle around the sentence that describes what happened last in the story.**

When children have finished Question 14, point out the stop sign at the bottom of the page. Explain that this sign means that children should stop what they are doing. They should not go on to the next page until they are told to do so. At this point, you may want to take a break. When children are ready, proceed with Part 2.

Questions 15–20

Make sure the children are on page 10. For questions 15 through 20, read the directions and the questions aloud.

Now we will be doing something different. Turn to page 10 in your test booklet. I will read a number and a sentence aloud. Find the number on your test page. Then look at the three words. I will read these three words aloud. Find the word that fits best in the sentence. Circle your answer.

Read the numbers and the questions below. Pause after each question to allow children to mark their answers.

15. **Joe asked the teacher for some . . . *what?* help . . . them . . . her? Circle your answer.**

16. **We sat in the shade under the big . . . *what?* eat . . . this . . . tree? Circle your answer.**

17. **When the teacher called her, Sara looked . . . *what?* from . . . use . . . up? Circle your answer.**

18. **When it is very cold, we must stay at . . . *what?* your . . . home . . . many? Circle your answer.**

19. **Lisa said, "I can't do it! It is . . . *what* hard!" too . . . take . . . on? Circle your answer.**

20. **We looked out the window and . . . *what* a rabbit. get . . . saw . . . way? Circle your answer.**

When children have finished Question 20, point out the stop sign at the bottom of the page. Explain that this sign means that children should stop what they are doing. They should not go on to the next page until they are told to do so.

READING – PART 3: PHONICS

Questions 21–34

Make sure children are on page 11. For questions 21 through 34, read the directions and the questions aloud.

Now we will be doing something different. Turn to page 11 in your test. Think about the story that we read about Ox and Bird. Now I will read a number and a question aloud. Find the number on your test page. Then look at the three words. Choose the word that best answers the question. Circle your answer.

Pause after each question to allow children to mark their answers.

21. **In this story, Ox asks if he <u>can</u> help. Which word has the same middle sound as *can . . . can?* Circle your answer.**

22. **In this story, Ox wants Bird to sit on a <u>rock</u>. Which word rhymes with *rock . . . rock?* Circle your answer.**

23. **One of the characters in this story is an <u>ox</u>. Which word rhymes with *ox . . . ox?* Circle your answer.**

24. **In this story, Bird sits on a <u>nest</u>. Which word has the same middle sound as *nest . . . nest?* Circle your answer.**

25. **In this story, Ox plays on the <u>rocks</u>. Which word rhymes with *rocks . . . rocks?* Circle your answer.**

Point out the Go On symbol and have children go on to the next page.

26. **Which word from the story tells about more than one thing? Circle the correct word.**

27. **In this story, Ox is <u>playing</u>. Which is the correct way to write *playing . . . playing?* Circle the correct word.**

28. **In this story, Ox is too <u>big</u>. Which word has the same middle sound as *big . . . big?* Circle your answer.**

29. **In this story, Ox wants to <u>play</u> with Bird. Which word has the same beginning sounds as *play . . . play?* Circle your answer.**

30. **In this story, Bird <u>must</u> stay on her nest. Which word has the same middle sound as *must . . . must?* Circle your answer.**

31. **In this story, Bird has a <u>nest</u>. Which word has the same ending sounds as *nest . . . nest?* Circle your answer.**

32. **In this story, Ox <u>sees</u> Bird. Which is the correct way to write *sees . . . sees?* Circle your answer.**

Benchmark Tests Teacher's Manual

33. In this story, Bird sits on a <u>nest</u>. Which word rhymes with *nest . . . nest?* Circle your answer.

34. In this story, Bird has to <u>sit</u> on her nest. Which word rhymes with *sit . . . sit?* Circle your answer.

When children have finished Question 34, point out the stop sign at the bottom of the page. Explain that this sign means that children should stop what they are doing. They should not go on to the next page until they are told to do so. At this point, you may want to take a break. When children are ready, proceed with Part 4.

READING – PART 4: WRITING CONVENTIONS

Questions 35–40

Make sure children are on page 14. For questions 35 through 40, read the directions and the questions aloud.

Now we will be doing something different. Turn to page 14 in your test. I will read a number and a question aloud. Find the number on your test page. Then look at the three answers. Choose the best answer for the question. Circle your answer.

Pause after each question to allow children to mark their answers.

35. **Which one is a sentence? Circle your answer.**

36. **Listen to this sentence. "The tree is green." What is the naming part? Circle your answer.**

37. **Listen to this sentence. "She runs home." What is the action part? Circle your answer.**

38. **Which one is in good word order? Circle your answer.**

39. **Which one is a telling sentence? Circle your answer.**

40. **Which one is an asking sentence? Circle your answer.**

When children have finished Question 40, point out the stop sign at the bottom of the page. Explain that this sign means that children should stop what they are doing. They should not go on to the next page until they are told to do so. At this point, you may want to take a break. When children are ready, proceed with Part 5.

WRITING – PART 5

Have children turn to page 16. Read the prompt aloud. Then read through the checklist for writers. Point out the lines on page 16 and make sure children know that they should write their responses on these lines. You may wish to give children scrap paper to use to plan their writing.

Now we will be doing something different. Turn to page 16 in your test. You are going to draw a picture and write about your picture.

Prompt:

In this story, Ox wanted to help Bird. Think of a time when you helped someone. It could be a person or an animal. Draw a picture of the time you helped someone. Then write one complete sentence about how you helped that person or animal.

Here are some things to remember when you are drawing and writing:

Checklist:

Plan your picture and sentence before you begin drawing and writing.

Check that your picture shows a time you helped someone.

Check that your sentence tells about a time you helped someone.

Begin your sentence with a capital letter.

End your sentence with an end mark.

Make sure your sentence makes sense.

Make sure the words are spelled correctly. If you are not sure how to spell a word, sound out the word and spell it as best you can.

Make sure your sentence is the way you want readers to read it.

Now draw a picture of the time you helped someone. Then write one complete sentence about how you helped that person or animal.

Give children 15 to 20 minutes to complete their activity.

DIRECTIONS – UNIT TEST 2

This is a test about reading and writing. In the first part, we will read a story and answer some questions about it. Open your test booklet to page 2.

READING – PART 1: COMPREHENSION

Selection: "Finding Dinner"

Directions in **bold** are to be read aloud; others are for your information only.

Read the directions on page 2 and have children read the story independently.

Directions: Little Bear wants dinner. Read the story to find out how Big Bear finds it. Then answer Numbers 1 through 14.

Now you are going to read the story. Then I will ask you some questions about the story. You may begin. Look up at me when you are finished reading.

[Note: If you feel that some of the children are not ready to read the story independently, you may read it aloud for those who need assistance.]

Questions 1–14

When children have finished reading the story, have them turn to page 6.

Now I am going to ask you some questions about the story. For each question, fill in the circle beside your answer. Listen carefully.

Make sure children are on page 6. For Questions 1 through 14, read each question number, the question, and the answer choices aloud. Pause after each question to allow children to mark their answers.

1. **Look at the question at the top of the page. What gave Big Bear wet feet? walking in the forest . . . hunting in the water . . . looking in the trees? Fill in the circle beside your answer.**

2. **What is this story all about? helping . . . walking . . . playing? Fill in the circle beside your answer.**

3. **What made Big Bear sad? He did not like the mice . . . He could not get honey . . . He could not find food? Fill in the circle beside your answer.**

4. **Big Bear got some honey. Then he went *where?* to the lake . . . to the forest . . . back home? Fill in the circle beside your answer.**

5. **The author wrote the story to tell about *what?* two bears . . . all animals . . . mice and fish? Fill in the circle beside your answer.**

6. What is a good name for this story? Big Bear Has Fun . . . Big Bear Helps Little Bear . . . Little Bear Is Sad? Fill in the circle beside your answer.

7. When there was no food, Big Bear had to *what?* get dinner . . . go out and play . . . get help? Fill in the circle beside your answer.

8. What did Big Bear want to do? grow food . . . play . . . find food? Fill in the circle beside your answer.

Point out the Go On symbol and have children go on to the next page.

9. The author wanted *what?* to make you safe in the forest . . . you to see Big Bear helping Little Bear . . . to tell you where to find honey? Fill in the circle beside your answer.

10. How can you tell this story is make-believe? Big Bear could talk . . . Big Bear looked for food . . . Little Bear liked honey. Fill in the circle beside your answer.

11. Where did Big Bear look for food last? in the lake . . . in the trees . . . in the park? Fill in the circle beside your answer.

12. At the end of the story, the author wanted you to *what?* eat your dinner . . . be sad . . . feel good? Fill in the circle beside your answer.

13. Where did this story take place? in a forest . . . in a lake . . . in a town? Fill in the circle beside your answer.

14. At the end of the story, Little Bear was *what?* sad . . . glad . . . mad? Fill in the circle beside your answer.

When children have finished Question 14, point out the stop sign at the bottom of the page. Explain that this sign means that children should stop what they are doing. They should not go on to the next page until they are told to do so. At this point, you may want to take a break. When children are ready, proceed with Part 2.

READING – PART 2: HIGH-FREQUENCY WORDS

Questions 15–20

Make sure children are on page 10. Read the directions and the questions aloud.

Now we will be doing something different. Turn to page 10 in your test booklet.

Directions: For Numbers 15 through 20, find the word that best fits in each sentence.

I will read the question number and the question aloud. Then I will read three words. Find the word that best fits into the sentence. Fill in the circle beside your answer. I will read the sentence twice.

Pause after each question to allow children to mark their answers.

15. The dog can not . . . *what* his bone. family . . . some . . . find . . . ? Fill in the circle beside your answer. The dog can not . . . *what* his bone.

16. It was cold. We . . . *what* not go to the zoo. could . . . new . . . put . . . ? Fill in the circle beside your answer. It was cold. We . . . *what* not go to the zoo.

17. Jane put seeds in the cage. The birds needed . . . *what?* good . . . food . . . grow . . . ? Fill in the circle beside your answer. The birds needed . . . *what?*

18. We all rode bikes . . . *what* the big park. also . . . around . . . people . . . ? Fill in the circle beside your answer. We all rode bikes . . . *what* the big park.

19. We wanted to go . . . *what*, but Mom said to play inside. out . . . under . . . horse . . . ? Fill in the circle beside your answer. We wanted to go . . . *what*, but Mom said to play inside.

20. Is . . . *what* a place you will let us play? now . . . old . . . there . . . ? Fill in the circle beside your answer. Is . . . *what* a place you will let us play?

When children have finished Question 20, point out the stop sign at the bottom of the page. Explain that this sign means that children should stop what they are doing. They should not go on to the next page until they are told to do so. Have children stop and listen while you read the directions for Numbers 21 through 34.

READING – PART 3: PHONICS

Questions 21–34

Make sure the children are on page 12. Read the directions and the questions aloud.

Now turn to page 12 in your test booklet.

Directions: For Numbers 21 through 34, listen to the question and fill in the circle under the correct answer.

I will read a question number, the sentence, and the question aloud. Find the word that best answers the question. Fill in the circle under your answer.

Pause after each question to allow children to mark their answers.

21. **In the story, Big Bear wanted to catch <u>fish</u>. Which word has the same ending sound as** *fish?* **Fill in the circle under your answer.**

22. **In this story, Big Bear <u>walked</u> around the forest. Which word rhymes with** *walked?* **Fill in the circle under your answer.**

23. **This story said, "<u>There</u> was no food." Which word has the same beginning sound as** *There?* **Fill in the circle under your answer.**

24. **In this story, Big Bear walks to the <u>lake</u>. Which word has the same middle sound as** *lake?* **Fill in the circle under your answer.**

25. **In this story, Big Bear can't find <u>mice</u>. Which word rhymes with** *mice?* **Fill in the circle under your answer.**

26. **In this story, Big Bear said he had a <u>place</u> to find animals. Which word has the same ending sound as** *place?* **Fill in the circle under your answer.**

27. **In this story, Big Bear wants to <u>chase</u> animals. Which word has the same beginning sound as** *chase?* **Fill in the circle under your answer.**

28. **In this story, Big Bear walked in a <u>huge</u> forest. Which word has the same ending sound as** *huge?* **Fill in the circle under your answer.**

29. **In this story, Big Bear went to <u>catch</u> mice. Which word has the same ending sound as** *catch?* **Fill in the circle under your answer.**

Point out the Go On symbol and have children go on to the next page.

30. **Big Bear said, "<u>I'll</u> go out." Which two words make up** *I'll?* **Fill in the circle under your answer.**

31. **At the end of the story Little Bear said, "<u>Thank</u> you," to Big Bear. Which word has the same beginning sound as** *thank?* **Fill in the circle under your answer.**

- -

32. This story said, "Then <u>he</u> looked for honey." Which word rhymes with *he?* Fill in the circle under your answer.

33. In this story, Big Bear ran <u>home</u>. Which word has the same middle sound as *home?* Fill in the circle under your answer.

34. In this story, Little Bear needed <u>dinner</u>. Which word has the same number of syllables as *dinner?* Fill in the circle under your answer.

When children have finished Question 34, point out the stop sign at the bottom of the page. Explain that this sign means that the children should stop what they are doing. They should not go on to the next page until they are told to do so. At this point, you may want to take a break. When children are ready, proceed with Part 4.

READING – PART 4: WRITING CONVENTIONS

Questions 35–40

Make sure children are on page 15. Read the directions and the questions aloud.

Now turn to page 15 in your test booklet.

Directions: For Numbers 35 through 40, find the one that is the best.

Pause after each question to allow children to mark their answers.

35. The . . . *what* is in the water. could . . . under . . . fish? Fill in the circle beside your answer.

36. There are four . . . *what* in the park. workers . . . worker . . . work? Fill in the circle beside your answer.

37. My cat Tom plays with mice. Which sentence is written correctly? Fill in the circle beside your answer.

Point out the Go On symbol and have children go on to the next page.

38. I like Mrs. Jones. Which sentence is written correctly? Fill in the circle beside your answer.

39. We play ball on Sunday. Which sentence is written correctly? Fill in the circle beside your answer.

40. It is hot in June. Which sentence is written correctly? Fill in the circle beside your answer.

When children have finished Question 40, point out the stop sign at the bottom of the page. Explain that this sign means that the children should stop what they are doing. They should not go on to the next page until they are told to do so. At this point, you may want to take a break. When children are ready, proceed with Part 5.

WRITING – PART 5

Have children turn to page 17. Read the prompt aloud. Then read through the checklist for writers. Point out the lines on page 18 and make sure children know that they should write their response on these lines. You may wish to give children scrap paper to use to plan their writing.

Prompt:

In "Finding Dinner," Little Bear wants to eat. Is there a sandwich that you like to eat best? How do you make this sandwich? Draw a picture of the sandwich you like to eat best. Then write to tell how to make the sandwich.

Here are some things to remember when you are drawing and writing:

Checklist:

Did I think about how to make the sandwich before I started writing?

Did I tell what steps to take to make it?

Did I put the steps in the right order?

Do my sentences make sense?

Do my sentences begin with capital letters?

Do my sentences end with end marks?

Did I check my spelling?

Did I make sure my paper is the way I want readers to read it?

Give children 15 to 20 minutes to complete their activity.

DIRECTIONS – UNIT TEST 3

This is a test about reading and writing. In the first part, we will read two stories and answer some questions about them. Open your test booklet to page 2.

READING – PART 1: COMPREHENSION

Selection 1: "Is It Spring?"

Directions in **bold** are to be read aloud; others are for your information only.

Open your test booklet to page 2. This first story is called "Is It Spring?"

When children are ready, read the directions on page 2 and have children read the story independently.

Directions: Many things start to happen in spring. Read about them. Then answer Numbers 1 through 7.

You may begin. Look up at me when you have finished reading.

[Note: If you feel that some of the children are not ready to read the story independently, you may read it aloud for those who need assistance.]

Questions 1–7

When children have finished reading the story, have them turn to page 6.

Now I am going to ask you some questions about the story. For each question, fill in the circle beside your answer.

Make sure children are on page 6. For Questions 1 through 7, read each question number and the question aloud.

[Note: If you feel that some children need additional assistance, you may also read the answer choices aloud from the test booklet.]

Pause after each question to allow children to mark their answers.

1. **Look at the question at the top of the page. What did Bird do at the end of the story? Fill in the circle beside your answer.**

2. **How are Raccoon, Bird, and Caterpillar the same? Fill in the circle beside your answer.**

3. **How are Bird and Caterpillar different? Fill in the circle beside your answer.**

4. **What did Raccoon do first? Fill in the circle beside your answer.**

5. **How did the animals know it was spring? Fill in the circle beside your answer.**

6. How can you tell this story is make-believe? Fill in the circle beside your answer.

7. In this story, the author wanted to . . . *do what?* Fill in the circle beside your answer.

Point out the stop sign at the bottom of the page. Explain that this sign means that children should stop what they are doing. They should not go on to the next page until they are told to do so. Have children stop and listen while you read the directions for Question A.

Now we are going to do something a little different. Make sure you are on page 8.

Directions: Write your answer to Question A on the lines below. Base your answer on the story "Is It Spring?"

A. Do you like spring? Tell why or why not.

Give children 5 minutes to write their answer to Question A.

When children have finished Question A, point out the stop sign at the bottom of the page. Explain that this sign means that children should stop what they are doing. They should not go on to the next page until they are told to do so. At this point, you may want to take a break. When children are ready, proceed with Passage 2.

Selection 2: "New Friends"

Open your test to page 9. This story is called "New Friends."

Read the directions on page 9 and have children read the story independently.

Directions: Moving to a new house can be hard. Read about Dan. Then answer Numbers 8 through 14.

You may begin. Look up at me when you have finished reading.

[Note: If you feel that some of the children are not ready to read the story independently, you may read it aloud for those who need assistance.]

Questions 8–14

When children have finished reading the story, have them turn to page 13.

Now I am going to ask you some questions about the story. For each question, fill in the circle beside your answer.

Make sure children are on page 13. For Questions 8 through 14, read each question number and the question aloud.

[Note: If you feel that some children need additional assistance, you may also read the answer choices aloud from the test booklet.]

Pause after each question to allow children to mark their answers.

8. **How did this story start? Fill in the circle beside your answer.**

9. **What did Dan do first? Fill in the circle beside your answer.**

10. **Why did Dan smile at the end? Fill in the circle beside your answer.**

11. **The big idea of this story is . . . what? Fill in the circle beside your answer.**

12. **What did Dan do last? Fill in the circle beside your answer.**

Point out the Go On symbol and have children go on to the next page.

13. **At the end of this story . . . *what happens?* Fill in the circle beside your answer.**

14. **How did Dan change in this story? Fill in the circle beside your answer.**

When children have finished Question 14, point out the stop sign at the bottom of the page. Explain that this sign means that children should stop what they are doing. They should not go on to the next page until they are told to do so. Have children stop and listen while you read the directions for Question B.

Now we are going to do something a little different. Make sure you are on page 15.

Directions: Write your answer to Question B on the lines below. Base your answer on the two stories you have read.

B. In the story "Is It Spring?" you met Raccoon. In the story "New Friends" you met Dan. How are Dan and Raccoon the same?

Give children five minutes to write their answer to Question B.

When children have finished Question B, point out the stop sign at the bottom of the page. Explain that this sign means that children should stop what they are doing. They should not go on to the next page until they are told to do so. At this point, you may want to take a break. When children are ready, proceed with Part 2.

Questions 15–20

Make sure children are on page 16. Read the directions and the questions aloud.

Directions: For Numbers 15 through 20, find the word that fits best in each sentence.

Pause after each question to allow children to mark their answers.

15. Mark takes the bus to . . . *what?* Fill in the circle beside your answer. Mark takes the bus to . . . *what?*

16. His family lives in a big . . . *what?* Fill in the circle beside your answer. His family lives in a big . . . *what?*

17. My grandmother lives far . . . *what?* Fill in the circle beside your answer. My grandmother lives far . . . *what?*

18. "Your hands are still dirty," said Dad. "You must wash them . . . *what?* Fill in the circle beside your answer. "Your hands are still dirty," said Dad. "You must wash them . . . *what?*

19. I did not eat any lunch. I hope Mother has dinner for us . . . *what?* Fill in the circle beside your answer. I did not eat any lunch. I hope Mother has dinner for us . . . *what?*

20. There is no rain. This is a good . . . *what* to play outside. Fill in the circle beside your answer. There is no rain. This is a good . . . *what* to play outside.

When children have finished Question 20, point out the stop sign at the bottom of the page. Explain that this sign means that children should stop what they are doing. They should not go on to the next page until they are told to do so. At this point, you may want to take a break. When children are ready, proceed with Part 3.

READING – PART 3: PHONICS

Questions 21–34

Make sure children are on page 18. Read the directions and the questions aloud.

Directions: For Numbers 21 through 34, fill in the circle under the correct answer.

Pause after each question to allow children to mark their answers.

21. It was <u>time</u> to eat dinner.

    What word has the same sound as the <u>i</u> in *time* . . . *time?*

22. The leaves were <u>very</u> green.

    What word has the same ending sound as *very* . . . *very?*

23. Soon <u>he</u> will be fat.

    What word rhymes with *he* . . . *he?*

24. Then he will become a beautiful butterfly.

    What word is made of two words put together?

25. It is <u>spring</u>.

    What word has the same ending sound as *spring* . . . *spring?*

26. Mother tells Dan to <u>go</u> to the park.

    What word rhymes with *go* . . . *go?*

27. The workers bring in <u>boxes</u>.

    What word has the same sound as the <u>es</u> in *boxes* . . . *boxes?*

28. Raccoon said

    Then I <u>think</u> it's spring.

    What word has the same ending sound as *think* . . . *think?*

29. Bird said

    It isn't cold any <u>more</u>.

    What word rhymes with *more* . . . *more?*

- - - - READING – PART 3: PHONICS - - - -

Point out the Go On symbol and have children go on to the next page.

30. **The animals know <u>it's</u> spring.**

    It's means . . . *what?*

31. **Caterpillar eats the <u>greenest</u> leaves.**

    The *greenest* leaves are . . . *what?*

32. **Dan plays in the <u>park</u>.**

    What word has the same middle sound as *park* . . . *park?*

33. **Caterpillar sees that it is not <u>raining</u> any more.**

    The rain has . . . *what?*

34. **Bill said**

    <u>We've</u> had fun.

    What two words make up *we've* . . . *we've?*

When children have finished Question 34, point out the stop sign at the bottom of
the page. Explain that this sign means that children should stop what they are doing.
They should not go on to the next page until they are told to do so. At this point,
you may want to take a break. When they are ready, have children listen while you
read the directions for Questions 35 through 40.

READING – PART 4: WRITING CONVENTIONS

Questions 35–40

Make sure children are on page 21. Read the directions and questions aloud.

Directions: Fill in the circle for your answers for Numbers 35 through 40.

Pause after each question to allow children to mark their answers.

35. **Which word is a verb? Fill in the circle beside your answer choice.**

36. **He . . . *what* the horse. Fill in the circle beside your answer choice.**

37. **They . . . *what* to go to the park. Fill in the circle beside your answer
    choice.**

38. **Which one tells what is happening now? Fill in the circle beside your
    answer choice.**

Point out the Go On symbol and have children go on to the next page.

39. **Which one tells what happened in the past? Fill in the circle beside your
    answer choice.**

Benchmark Tests Teacher's Manual

40. Which sentence is written correctly? Fill in the circle beside your answer choice.

When children have finished Question 40, point out the stop sign at the bottom of the page. Explain that this sign means that children should stop what they are doing. They should not go on to the next page until they are told to do so. At this point, you may want to take a break. When children are ready, proceed with Part 5.

WRITING – PART 5

Have children turn to page 23. Read the prompt aloud. Then read through the checklist for writers. Tell children to make a checkmark next to each step after they finish the task. Point out the lines on page 24 and make sure children know that they should write their response on these lines. You may wish to give them scrap paper to use to plan their writing.

Prompt:

In "Is It Spring?" the animals see flowers growing. Think of what it's like outside in the spring. Write to tell what spring is like.

Checklist:

Did I think about spring before I started to write?

Did I tell what spring is like?

Did I use sense words to tell about things I can see, hear, smell, taste, or touch in the spring?

Do my sentences make sense?

Do my sentences begin with capital letters?

Do my sentences end with end marks?

Did I check my spelling?

Did I make sure my paper is the way I want readers to read it?

Give children 15 to 20 minutes to complete this activity.

DIRECTIONS – UNIT TEST 4

This is a test about reading and writing. In the first part, we will read two stories and answer some questions about them.

READING – PART 1: COMPREHENSION

Selection 1: "A Wonderful Friend"

Directions in **bold** are to be read aloud; others are for your information only.

Open your test booklet to page 2. This first story is called "A Wonderful Friend."

When children are ready, read the directions on page 2, and have children read the story independently.

Directions: Sometimes friends must say good-bye. Read this story about two friends. Then answer Numbers 1 through 7.

You may begin. Look up at me when you have finished reading.

[Note: If you feel that some of the children are not ready to read the story independently, you may read it aloud for those who need assistance.]

Questions 1–7

When children have finished reading the story, have them turn to page 6.

Now I am going to ask you some questions about the story. For each question, fill in the circle beside your answer.

Make sure children are on page 6. For Questions 1 through 7, read each question number and the question aloud.

[Note: If you feel that some children need additional assistance, you may also read the answer choices aloud from the test booklet.]

Pause after each question to allow children to mark their answers.

1. **Look at the question on the top of the page. Why did Pam's family have to go away? Fill in the circle beside your answer.**

2. **The author wrote this story to tell you . . . *what?* Fill in the circle beside your answer.**

3. **Why did Lee give Pam a present? Fill in the circle beside your answer.**

4. **What can you tell about Pam and Lee? Fill in the circle beside your answer.**

5. **What does this story teach us? Fill in the circle beside your answer.**

6. **What can you tell about Pam's mother? Fill in the circle beside your answer.**

7. **What happened at the end of this story? Fill in the circle beside your answer.**

Point out the stop sign at the bottom of the page. Explain that this sign means that children should stop what they are doing. They should not go on to the next page until they are told to do so. Have children stop and listen while you read the directions to Question A.

Now we are going to do something a little different. Make sure you are on page 8.

Directions: Write your answer to Question A on the lines below. Base your answer on "A Wonderful Friend."

A. **In "A Wonderful Friend," Lee's friend Pam has to move away. Tell how you would feel if a good friend had to move away. Tell what present you would give your friend.**

Give children 5 minutes to write their answer to Question A.

When children have finished Question A, point out the stop sign at the bottom of the page. Explain that this sign means that children should stop what they are doing. They should not go on to the next page until they are told to do so. At this point, you may want to take a break. When children are ready, proceed with Passage 2.

Selection 2: "How to Be a Hummingbird's Friend"

Directions in **bold** are to be read aloud; others are for your information only.

Turn your test booklet to page 9. This is a story called "How to Be a Hummingbird's Friend."

When children are ready, read the directions on page 9 and have children read the story independently.

Directions: Read about how to help a hurt hummingbird. Then answer Numbers 8 through 14.

You may begin. Look up at me when you have finished reading.

[Note: If you feel that some of the children are not ready to read the story independently, you may read it aloud for those who need assistance.]

Questions 8–14

When children have finished reading the story, have them turn to page 13.

Now I am going to ask some questions about the story. For each question, fill in the circle beside your answer.

Make sure children are on page 13. For Questions 8 through 14, read each question number and the question aloud.

[Note: If you feel that some children need additional assistance, you may also read the answer choices aloud from the test booklet.]

Pause after each question to allow children to mark their answers.

8. **What should you do first if you find a hurt hummingbird? Fill in the circle beside your answer.**

9. **What does this story teach us about? Fill in the circle beside your answer.**

10. **Which of these statements is an opinion? Fill in the circle beside your answer.**

11. **The author wrote "How to Be a Hummingbird's Friend" to tell . . . *what?* Fill in the circle beside your answer.**

12. **A hummingbird might be afraid of you because . . . *why?* Fill in the circle beside your answer.**

13. **How can you keep a hummingbird warm? Fill in the circle beside your answer.**

14. **Which of these statements is an opinion? Fill in the circle beside your answer.**

Point out the stop sign at the bottom of the page. Explain that this sign means that children should stop what they are doing. They should not go on to the next page until they are told to do so. Have children stop and listen while you read the directions for Question B.

Now we are going to do something a little different. Make sure you are on page 15.

Directions: Write your answer to Question B on the lines below. Base your answer on the two stories you have read.

B. **Both "A Wonderful Friend" and "How to Be a Hummingbird's Friend" are about friends. How are the friends in these stories different?**

Give children 5 minutes to write their answer to Question B.

When children have finished Question B, point out the stop sign at the bottom of the page. Explain that this sign means that children should stop what they are doing. They should not go on to the next page until they are told to do so. At this point, you may want to take a break. When children are ready, proceed with Part 2.

READING – PART 2: HIGH-FREQUENCY WORDS

Questions 15–20

Make sure children are on page 16. Read the directions and the questions aloud.

Directions: Fill in the circle beside your answer choice for Numbers 15 through 20.

Pause after each question to allow children to mark their answers.

15. Tim liked art. He . . . *what* . . . beautiful pictures. Fill in the circle beside your answer choice. He . . . *what* . . . beautiful pictures.

16. "Your dance will be great," said Father. "Don't . . . *what* . . . at all." Fill in the circle beside your answer choice. "Don't . . . *what* . . . at all."

17. The girls like games. They . . . *what* . . . playing Go Fish. Fill in the circle beside your answer choice. They . . . *what* . . . playing Go Fish.

18. We had a gift for Mom. It was a . . . *what*. Fill in the circle beside your answer choice. It was a . . . *what*.

19. A hummingbird is not a pet. It is a . . . *what* . . . animal. Fill in the circle beside your answer choice. It is a . . . *what* . . . animal.

20. "Is that a new book?" asked Dad. "Will you . . . *what* . . . it to me?" Fill in the circle beside your answer choice. "Will you . . . *what* . . . it to me?"

Point out the stop sign at the bottom of the page. Explain that this sign means that children should stop what they are doing. They should not go on to the next page until they are told to do so. At this point, you may want to take a break. When children are ready, proceed with Part 3.

READING – PART 3: PHONICS

Questions 21–34

Make sure children are on page 18. Read the directions and the questions aloud.

Directions: For Numbers 21 through 34, fill in the circle under the correct answer.

Pause after each question to allow time for children to mark their answers.

21. Lee and Pam <u>play</u> in the park.

    What word rhymes with *play . . . play?*

22. Pam's mother helps birds <u>grow</u>.

    What word has the same sound as the <u>ow</u> in *grow . . . grow?*

23. Lee and Pam like to draw and <u>read</u>.

    What word has the same sound as the <u>ea</u> in *read . . . read?*

24. Pam <u>sighs</u> when she gets a present.

    What word has the same sound as the <u>igh</u> in *sighs . . . sighs?*

25. Lee said

    I will write to you <u>soon</u>.

    What word has the same sound as the <u>oo</u> in *soon . . . soon?*

26. Pam said

    Be sure to <u>write</u>.

    What word has the same beginning sound as *write . . . write?*

27. Find the word that is best in the sentence.

    What . . . mother has a new job.

28. Hummingbirds are <u>beautiful</u>.

    The word *beautiful* means . . .

29. They have shiny red and <u>blue</u> feathers.

    What word rhymes with *blue . . . blue?*

Point out the Go On symbol and have children go on to the next page.

30. A hummingbird does not <u>know</u> you are its friend.

    What word has the same beginning sound as *know . . . know?*

31. **You cannot do anything more to help it.**

   What word is a compound word?

32. **Hummingbirds have beautiful <u>feathers</u>.**

   What word has the same sound as the <u>ea</u> in *feathers . . . feathers?*

33. **The hummingbird may be <u>afraid</u>.**

   What word has the same sound as the <u>ai</u> in *afraid . . . afraid?*

34. **Pick up the hummingbird <u>slowly</u>.**

   What means the same as *slowly . . . slowly?*

Point out the stop sign at the bottom of the page. Explain that this sign means that children should stop what they are doing. They should not go on to the next page until they are told to do so. Have children stop and listen while you read the directions for Part 4.

READING – PART 4: WRITING CONVENTIONS

Questions 35–40

Make sure children are on page 21. Read the directions and questions aloud.

Directions: Fill in the circle for your answer choice for Numbers 35 through 40.

Pause after each question to allow children to mark their answers.

35. **What word in this sentence tells about the bird's feathers?**

   The bird has green feathers. Fill in the circle beside your answer choice.

36. **What word in this sentence tells about the tree?**

   The pretty bird flew quickly to the big tree. Fill in the circle beside your answer choice.

37. **What word in this sentence tells how many girls?**

   Nine little girls play under the tall tree. Fill in the circle beside your answer choice.

Point out the Go On symbol and have children go on to the next page.

38. **What word in this sentence is a describing word?**

   The friends sang their sad song. Fill in the circle next to your answer.

Find the word that best fits in each sentence.

39. The baby is the . . . *what* . . . one in their family.

    Fill in the circle beside your answer choice.

40. The boy is . . . *what* . . . than the hummingbird.

    Fill in the circle beside your answer choice.

Point out the stop sign at the bottom of the page. Explain that this sign means that children should stop what they are doing. They should not go on to the next page until they are told to do so. At this point, you may want to take a break. When children are ready, proceed with Part 5.

WRITING – PART 5

Have children turn to page 23. Read the prompt aloud. Then read through the checklist for writers. Tell children to make a checkmark next to each step after they finish the task. Point out the lines on page 24 and make sure children know that they should write their response on these lines. You may wish to give them scrap paper to use to plan their writing.

Prompt:

Pretend your good friend went to live in a new town. You would like to see your friend again. Write a letter to your friend. Ask your friend to come visit you.

Tell your friend all the good reasons to come for a visit. Write at least three sentences.

Checklist:

Did I pretend that a good friend went to live in a new town?

Did I ask my friend to come visit me?

Did I tell why my friend should visit me?

Did I write at least three sentences?

Did I sign my letter?

Do my sentences make sense?

Do my sentences begin with capital letters?

Do my sentences end with end marks?

Did I check my spelling?

Did I make sure my letter is the way I want readers to read it?

Give children 15 to 20 minutes to complete this activity.

DIRECTIONS – UNIT TEST 5

This is a test about reading and writing. In the first part, we will read two stories and answer some questions about them.

READING – PART 1: COMPREHENSION

Selection 1: "A Rainy Day"

Directions in **bold** are to be read aloud; others are for your information only.

Open your test booklet to page 2. This first story is called "A Rainy Day."

When children are ready, read the directions on page 2, and have children read the story independently.

Directions: Two friends can make a rainy day fun. Learn what Dan and Joy
do while it is raining. Then answer Numbers 1 through 7.

You may begin. Look up at me when you have finished reading.

Questions 1–7

When children have finished reading the story, have them turn to page 5. Have children complete Numbers 1 through 7 on their own.

Now you are going to answer some questions about the story. For each question, fill in the circle beside your answer.

[Note: If children have difficulty reading the questions, you may assist them as needed.]

Point out the stop sign at the bottom of page 6. Explain that they are not to go on to the next page until they are told to do so.

When children have finished Number 7, have them turn to page 7 and look at Question A. Make sure children understand that they should write the answer to Question A on the lines in their tests. Encourage children to use words from the story in their answer, to write complete sentences, and to check their sentences when they are done. Read the directions on page 7. Have children complete Question A on their own.

Directions: Write your answer to Question A on the lines below. Base your answer on the story "A Rainy Day."

[Note: If children seem to have difficulty reading Question A, you may assist them as needed.]

Give children 5 minutes to write their answer to Question A.

When children have finished Question A, point out the stop sign at the bottom of the page. Explain that this sign means that children should stop what they are doing. They should not go on to the next page until they are told to do so. At this point, you may want to take a break. When children are ready, proceed with Selection 2.

Selection 2: "A Farmer's Life"

Directions in **bold** are to be read aloud; others are for your information only.

Turn your test booklet to page 8. This story is called "A Farmer's Life."

When children are ready, read the directions on page 8 and have children read the story independently.

Directions: Have you ever wondered what a farmer does? Read "A Farmer's Life" and find out. Then answer Numbers 8 through 14.

You may begin. Look up at me when you have finished reading.

Questions 8–14

When children have finished reading, make sure they are on page 12. Have children complete Numbers 8 through 14 on their own.

For each question, fill in the circle beside your answer.

[Note: If children have difficulty reading the questions, you may assist them as needed.]

Point out the stop sign at the bottom of page 13. Explain that they are not to go on to the next page until told to do so.

When children have finished Number 14, have them turn to page 14. Read the directions on page 14. Have children complete Question B on their own. Make sure they understand that they should use words from both passages in their answer.

Directions: Write your answer to Question B on the lines below. Base your answer on the two selections you have read.

[Note: You may assist children with Question B as needed.]

Give children 5 minutes to write their answer to Question B.

When children have finished Question B, point out the stop sign at the bottom of the page. Explain that this sign means that children should stop what they are doing. They should not go on to the next page until they are told to do so. At this point, you may want to take a break. When children are ready, proceed with Part 2.

READING – PART 2: HIGH-FREQUENCY WORDS

Questions 15–20

Make sure children are on page 15. Read the directions aloud.

Directions: For Numbers 15 through 20, find the word that best fits in each sentence.

When children have finished questions 15 through 20, point out the stop sign at the bottom of the page. Explain that this sign means that children should stop what they are doing. They should not go on to the next page until they are told to do so. At this point, you may want to take a break. When children are ready, proceed with Part 3.

READING – PART 3: PHONICS

Questions 21–34

Make sure children are on page 17. Read the directions aloud.

Directions: For Numbers 21 through 34, find the answer to each question.

[Note: If children have difficulty reading the questions, you may assist them as needed.]

Point out the stop sign at the bottom of page 20. Explain that this sign means that children should stop what they are doing. They should not go on to the next page until they are told to do so. At this point, you may want to take a break. When children are ready, proceed with Part 4.

READING – PART 4: WRITING CONVENTIONS

Questions 35–40

Make sure children are on page 21. Read the directions aloud.

Directions: Fill in the circle beside your answer choice for Numbers 35 through 40.

[Note: If children have difficulty reading the questions, you may assist them as needed.]

Point out the stop sign at the bottom of page 22. Explain that this sign means that children should stop what they are doing. They should not go on to the next page until they are told to do so. At this point, you may want to take a break. When children are ready, proceed with Part 5.

WRITING – PART 5

Have children turn to page 23. Point out the lines on page 24 and make sure children know that they should write their response on these lines. Tell children to make a checkmark next to each step in the checklist for writers. You may wish to give them scrap paper to use to plan their writing.

Prompt:

What do you like to do when you have free time? Do you like to be inside or outside? Why? Write at least three sentences to tell what you like to do when you have free time.

Checklist:

Did I plan my paper before I started writing?

Did I say why I like to be inside or outside?

Did I say what I like to do when I have free time?

Do my sentences make sense?

Do my sentences begin with capital letters?

Do my sentences end with end marks?

Did I check my spelling?

Did I make sure my paper is the way I want readers to read it?

Give children 15 to 20 minutes to complete this activity.

DIRECTIONS – END-OF-YEAR TEST

This is a test about reading and writing. In the first part, we will read three stories and answer some questions about them.

READING – PART 1: COMPREHENSION

Selection 1: "Where Is Bear?"

Directions in **bold** are to be read aloud; others are for your information only.

Open your test booklet to page 2. This first story is called "Where Is Bear?"

When children are ready, read the directions on page 2 and have children read the story independently.

Directions: Paco's favorite toy is missing! Read about how Paco's sister and mother look for the toy. Then answer Numbers 1 through 7.

You may begin. Look up at me when you have finished reading.

Questions 1–7

When children are finished reading the story, have them turn to page 6 and complete Numbers 1 through 7 on their own.

Now turn to page 6. You are going to answer Numbers 1 through 7. Read the question, and then fill in the circle beside the best answer to each question. Look up at me when you have finished Number 7.

[Note: If children have difficulty reading the questions, you may assist them as needed.]

Point out the stop sign at the bottom of page 7. Explain that they are not to go on to the next page until they are told to do so.

Selection 2: "The Hale Boys Build a Car"

Directions in **bold** are to be read aloud; others are for your information only.

Let's go on to the second story. Turn to page 8 of your test.

This story is called "The Hale Boys Build a Car."

When children are ready, read the directions on page 8 and have children read the story independently.

Directions: Read about two brothers who love cars. Then answer Numbers 8 through 14.

You may begin. Look up at me when you are finished reading.

When children are finished reading the story, have them turn to page 12 and complete the answers to Questions 8 through 14.

Questions 8–14

Now turn to page 12. You will answer Numbers 8 through 14. Read the question, and then fill in the circle beside the best answer to each question. Look up at me when you have finished Number 14.

[Note: If children have difficulty reading the questions, you may assist them as needed.]

When children have finished Number 14, have them turn to page 14 and look at Question A. Make sure children understand that they should write the answer to Question A on the lines in their tests. Encourage children to use words from the stories in their answer, to write complete sentences, and to check their sentences when they are done. Read the directions on page 14. Have children complete Question A on their own.

Directions: Write your answer to Question A on the lines below. Base your answer on the two stories you have read.

[Note: You may assist children with Question A as needed.]

Give children 5 minutes to write their answer to Question A.

At this point, you may want to take a break. When children are ready, proceed with the next activity.

Selection 3: "Riding a Horse"

Directions in **bold** are to be read aloud; others are for your information only.

Let's go on to the third selection. Turn to page 15 of your test.

This selection is called "Riding a Horse."

When children are ready, read the directions on page 15 and have children read the selection independently.

Directions: Do you like horses? Read this to learn about riding a horse. Then answer Numbers 15 through 21.

You may begin. Look up at me when you have finished reading.

When children are finished reading, have them turn to page 18 and complete the answers to Questions 15 through 21 on their own.

Questions 15–21

Now turn to page 18. You will answer Numbers 15 through 21. Read the question, then fill in the circle beside the best answer to each question. Look up at me when you have finished Number 21.

[Note: If children have difficulty reading the questions, you may assist them as needed.]

When children have finished Number 21, have them turn to page 20. Read the directions on page 20. Have children complete Question B on their own. Make sure they understand that they should use words from both selections in their answer.

Directions: Write your answer to Question B on the lines below. Base your answer on "The Hale Boys Build a Car" and "Riding a Horse."

Give children 5 minutes to write their answer to Question B.

[Note: You may assist children with Question B as needed.]

Point out the stop sign at the bottom of page 20. Explain that they are not to go on to the next page until told to do so.

At this point, you may want to take a break. When children are ready, proceed with the next activity.

READING – PART 2: HIGH-FREQUENCY WORDS

Questions 22–30

Make sure children are on page 21. Read the directions aloud.

Directions: Fill in the circle below your answer choice for Numbers 22 through 30.

When children have finished Questions 22 through 30, point out the stop sign at the bottom of the page. Explain that this sign means that children should stop what they are doing. They should not go on to the next page until they are told to do so.

READING – PART 3: PHONICS

Questions 31–51

Make sure children are on page 23. Read the directions aloud.

Directions: For Numbers 31 through 51, mark the answer to each question.

Point out the stop sign at the bottom of page 27. Explain that this sign means that children should stop what they are doing. They should not go on to the next page until they are told to do so.

READING – PART 4: WRITING CONVENTIONS

Questions 52–60

Make sure children are on page 28. Read the directions aloud.

Directions: Fill in the circle for your answer choice for Numbers 52 through 60.

Point out the stop sign at the bottom of page 29. Explain that this sign means that children should stop what they are doing. They should not go on to the next page until they are told to do so. At this point, you may want to take a break. When children are ready, proceed with Part 5.

WRITING – PART 5

Have children turn to page 30. Point out the lines on page 31 and make sure children know that they should write their response on these lines. Tell children to make a checkmark next to each step in the checklist for writers. You may wish to give them scrap paper to use to plan their writing.

Prompt:

In "The Hale Boys Build a Car" and "Riding a Horse," the children become old enough to do something new. Think about something new that you have learned to do this year. Write a story about a new thing you did this year. Tell how it made you feel.

Checklist:

Did I plan my story before I started writing?

Does my story tell about something new I learned to do this year?

Does my story tell how doing something new made me feel?

Does my story have a beginning, middle, and end?

Does my story make sense?

Do my sentences begin with capital letters?

Do my sentences end with end marks?

Did I check my spelling?

Did I make sure my paper is the way I want readers to read it?

Give children about 30 minutes to complete this activity.

ANSWER KEYS

Unit 1 Benchmark Test

Reading – Part 1: Comprehension

Selection: "Ox and Bird"

1. second picture (Ox playing on the rocks)
2. first picture (Bird sitting on a nest in a tree)
3. second picture (Bird sitting on nest)
4. second choice (She had to sit on the nest.)
5. first picture (sunny day)
6. third choice (A bird said to go home.)
7. first picture (Bird watching baby hatching)
8. first choice (on the rocks)
9. first choice (He is too big.)
10. third choice (Ox Can Not Help)
11. first choice (help Bird)
12. third picture (angry face)
13. second picture (sad face)
14. second choice (Bird said to go home.)

Reading – Part 2: High-Frequency Words

15. first choice (help)
16. third choice (tree)
17. third choice (up)
18. second choice (home)
19. first choice (too)
20. second choice (saw)

Reading – Part 3: Phonics

21. second choice (tap)
22. third choice (sock)
23. first choice (fox)
24. third choice (let)
25. second choice (locks)
26. second choice (rocks)
27. first choice (playing)
28. third choice (dig)
29. first choice (plan)
30. first choice (rub)
31. second choice (rust)
32. first choice (sees)
33. third choice (best)
34. second choice (pit)

Reading – Part 4: Writing Conventions

35. first choice (She sees the trees.)
36. third choice (The tree)
37. first choice (runs)
38. second choice (The bird sits on the nest.)
39. first choice (I like to play in the park.)
40. third choice (Where do the zebras play?)

Writing – Part 5

Prompt: Children are asked to draw a picture of a time they helped someone and write a sentence describing how they helped that person or animal.

Scoring: Assess children's drawing based on how well the drawing addresses the suggested task and its level of detail. Assess children's writing based on how well it relates to the drawing and its use of appropriate writing conventions. Use one of the Narrative Writing Scoring Rubrics on pages T11–T12 to help you assess children's compositions. Choose one of the four rubrics, and assign each composition a score based on the 6-point, 5-point, 4-point, or 3-point scale.

Unit 2 Benchmark Test

Reading – Part 1: Comprehension

Selection: "Finding Dinner"

1. second choice (hunting in the water)
2. first choice (helping)
3. third choice (He could not find food.)
4. third choice (back home.)
5. first choice (two bears.)
6. second choice (Big Bear Helps Little Bear)
7. first choice (get dinner.)
8. third choice (find food)
9. second choice (you to see Big Bear helping Little Bear.)
10. first choice (Big Bear could talk.)
11. second choice (in the trees)
12. third choice (feel good.)
13. first choice (in a forest)
14. second choice (glad.)

Reading – Part 2: High-Frequency Words

15. third choice (find)
16. first choice (could)
17. second choice (food)
18. second choice (around)
19. first choice (out)
20. third choice (there)

Reading – Part 3: Phonics

21. second choice (wish)
22. first choice (talked)
23. third choice (they)
24. first choice (made)
25. third choice (nice)
26. second choice (rice)
27. third choice (chin)
28. first choice (page)
29. second choice (witch)
30. third choice (I will)
31. first choice (third)
32. second choice (bee)
33. first choice (bone)
34. first choice (picnic)

Reading – Part 4: Writing Conventions

35. third choice (fish)
36. first choice (workers)
37. second choice (My cat Tom plays with mice.)
38. first choice (I like Mrs. Jones.)
39. third choice (We play ball on Sunday.)
40. second choice (It is hot in June.)

Writing – Part 5

Prompt: Children are asked to draw a picture of a sandwich and write to tell how to make the sandwich.

Scoring: Assess children's drawing based on how well the drawing addresses the suggested task and its level of detail. Assess children's writing based on how well it relates to the drawing and its use of appropriate writing conventions. Use one of the Expository Writing Scoring Rubrics on pages T15–T16 to help you assess children's compositions. Choose one of the four rubrics, and assign each composition a score based on the 6-point, 5-point, 4-point, or 3-point scale.

Unit 3 Benchmark Test

Reading – Part 1: Comprehension

Selection 1: "Is It Spring?"

1. second choice (She looked for a place for a nest.)
2. first choice (They are all happy it is spring.)
3. third choice (Bird needs to make a nest.)
4. second choice (He looked out from the tree.)
5. third choice (They saw flowers.)
6. first choice (The animals talked.)
7. third choice (tell you what animals do in the spring.)

A. Use the Constructed-Response Scoring Rubric on page T10 to help you assess children's responses. Assign a score from 0 to 2.

Possible top response: I like spring because the weather changes. It goes from cold and snowy to warm and sunny. I do not have to wear a heavy jacket.

Selection 2: "New Friends"

8. second choice (Dan came to a new house.)
9. third choice (He watched the workers.)
10. first choice (He was glad to have a new friend.)
11. third choice (finding new friends.)
12. first choice (He came home.)
13. second choice (Dan was happy he had friends.)
14. first choice (First he was sad, and then he was happy.)

B. Use the Constructed-Response Scoring Rubric on page T10 to help you assess children's responses. Assign a score from 0 to 2.

Possible top response: Both are looking for friends. Raccoon finds friends because it is spring. Dan finds new friends at his new school.

Reading – Part 2: High-Frequency Words

15. third choice (school)
16. second choice (house)
17. first choice (away)
18. first choice (again)
19. second choice (soon)
20. third choice (day)

Reading – Part 3: Phonics

21. third choice (why)
22. second choice (penny)
23. first choice (tree)
24. second choice (butterfly)
25. third choice (wing)

26. first choice (no)

27. third choice (dishes)

28. second choice (bank)

29. first choice (store)

30. second choice (it is.)

31. first choice (the most green.)

32. third choice (dart)

33. second choice (stopped.)

34. third choice (we have)

Reading – Part 4: Writing Conventions

35. first choice (eat)

36. third choice (rides)

37. third choice (want)

38. first choice (She looks at the ground.)

39. second choice (We walked to school.)

40. third choice (They won't come inside.)

Writing – Part 5

Prompt: Children are asked to tell what spring is like.

Scoring: Use one of the Descriptive Writing Scoring Rubrics on pages T13–T14 to help you assess children's compositions. Choose one of the four rubrics, and assign each composition a score based on the 6-point, 5-point, 4-point, or 3-point scale.

Unit 4 Benchmark Test

Reading – Part 1: Comprehension

Selection 1: "A Wonderful Friend"

1. first choice (Pam's mother had a new job.)

2. first choice (something about friends.)

3. third choice (Lee liked Pam.)

4. second choice (They liked to be together.)

5. third choice (It is good to have friends.)

6. second choice (She liked birds.)

7. first choice (Lee and Pam said good-bye.)

A. Use the Constructed-Response Scoring Rubric on page T10 to help you assess children's responses. Assign a score from 0 to 2.

Possible top response: I would feel sad if my friend Sue moved away. I would miss her at school. I would give her a book for a present. Maybe I could visit her one day.

Selection 2: "How to Be a Hummingbird's Friend."

8. first choice (Pick it up slowly.)

9. third choice (helping.)

10. second choice (Hummingbirds are beautiful.)

11. third choice (how to take care of a hurt hummingbird.)

12. first choice (it is a wild animal.)

13. second choice (Place it in a box.)

14. first choice (It is good that you were the hummingbird's friend.)

B. Use the Constructed-Response Scoring Rubric on page T10 to help you assess children's responses. Assign a score from 0 to 2.

Responses may vary. Possible top response: In the first story the friends are people. They will always be friends. In the second story a person learns how to help an animal. The person and animal will not see each other again.

Reading – Part 2: High-Frequency Words

15. second choice (drew)
16. first choice (worry)
17. third choice (enjoy)
18. second choice (surprise)
19. first choice (wild)
20. third choice (show)

Reading – Part 3: Phonics

21. first choice (stay)
22. third choice (boat)
23. second choice (meat)
24. first choice (ride)
25. third choice (fruit)
26. third choice (room)
27. second choice (Pam's)
28. third choice (full of beauty.)
29. first choice (flew)
30. first choice (need)
31. first choice (anything)
32. third choice (bread)
33. third choice (made)
34. second choice (in a slow way)

Reading – Part 4: Writing Conventions

35. third choice (green)
36. third choice (big)
37. first choice (nine)
38. third choice (sad)
39. first choice (smallest)
40. first choice (bigger)

Writing – Part 5

Prompt: Children are asked to write a letter to a friend telling a friend why he or she should visit. Letter to contain at least three sentences and a closing signature.

Scoring: Use one of the Persuasive Writing Scoring Rubrics on pages T17–T18 to help you assess children's compositions. Choose one of the four rubrics, and assign each composition a score based on the 6-point, 5-point, 4-point, or 3-point scale.

Unit 5 Benchmark Test

Reading – Part 1: Comprehension

Selection 1: "A Rainy Day"

1. third choice (inside)
2. first choice (Friends can always have a good time together.)
3. second choice (He did not want to be inside.)
4. third choice (how to have fun)
5. second choice (Dan and Joy saw that it was raining.)
6. first choice (two friends)
7. third choice (She could have fun even on a rainy day.)

A. Use the Constructed-Response Scoring Rubric on page T10 to help you assess children's responses. Assign a score from 0 to 2.

Possible top response: On a rainy day I like to bake cookies, watch TV, and play race cars with my little brother.

Selection 2: "A Farmer's Life"

  8. third choice (oats)

  9. second choice (They are made into oatmeal.)

10. first choice (teach real things.)

11. third choice (sheep and goats)

12. first choice (what farmers do)

13. second choice (get up early in the morning)

14. first choice (Their crops and animals are outside.)

B. Use the Constructed-Response Scoring Rubric on page T10 to help you assess children's responses. Assign a score from 0 to 2.

Answers may vary. Possible top response: I think Dan would like spending a day outside on a farm. He was not happy to be inside when it was raining. He would have fun being outside.

Reading – Part 2: High-Frequency Words

15. first choice (early)

16. third choice (eyes)

17. second choice (answered)

18. third choice (different)

19. first choice (another)

20. second choice (among)

Reading – Part 3: Phonics

21. first choice (paper)

22. third choice (count)

23. second choice (not happy)

24. third choice (toy)

25. second choice (saw)

26. first choice (loved)

27. third choice (using)

28. second choice (finds)

29. first choice (people who work on farms)

30. third choice (oatmeal)

31. third choice (how)

32. first choice (cat • tle)

33. second choice (post)

34. first choice (book)

Reading – Part 4: Writing Conventions

35. second choice (me)

36. first choice (I)

37. second choice (Next)

38. first choice (you)

39. second choice (they)

40. third choice (Go to school.)

Writing – Part 5

Prompt: Children are asked to write at least three sentences about how they like to spend their free time.

Scoring: Use one of the Descriptive Writing Scoring Rubrics on pages T13–T14 to help you assess children's compositions. Choose one of the four rubrics, and assign each composition a score based on the 6-point, 5-point, 4-point, or 3-point scale.

End-of-Year Benchmark Test

Reading – Part 1: Comprehension

Selection 1: "Where Is Bear?"

1. second choice (at their house)
2. first choice (Paco had Bear the whole time.)
3. third choice (Bear could run and play.)
4. second choice ("Rosa Finds Bear")
5. second choice (in the playroom)
6. third choice (helping her mother.)
7. first choice (Rosa found Bear.)

Selection 2: "The Hale Boys Build a Car"

8. second choice (Mike and Adam drew cars on paper.)
9. third choice (nice)
10. first choice (He knew they loved cars.)
11. second choice (Two brothers build a car with their father.)
12. first choice (be happy for these boys.)
13. second choice (many weeks)
14. third choice (You can make great things when you work together.)

A. Use the Constructed-Response Scoring Rubric on page T10 to help you assess children's responses. Assign each response a score from 0 to 2.

Possible top response:
Rosa and the Hale boys' father both help people in their family find or make something their family members like, even if it was not something they liked too.

Selection 3: "Riding a Horse"

15. third choice (And riding a horse is fun!)
16. second choice (make friends with the horse)
17. first choice (trust each other.)
18. third choice (the horse will get to know you.)
19. second choice (getting to know a dog.)
20. first choice (ride it.)
21. first choice (how you learn to ride a horse.)

B. Use the Constructed-Response Scoring Rubric on page T10 to help you assess children's responses. Assign each response a score from 0 to 2.

Answers will vary. A possible top response might be: I would like to ride a horse because I love horses. I like being in the country instead of being in a car in the city.

Reading – Part 2: High-Frequency Words

22. third choice (answered)
23. second choice (eight)
24. first choice (laughed)
25. first choice (enough)
26. second choice (people)
27. third choice (thought)
28. first choice (friends)
29. second choice (sign)
30. third choice (great)

Reading – Part 3: Phonics

31. first choice (join)

32. second choice (sleep)

33. third choice (chase)

34. first choice (did not)

35. second choice (sleep)

36. third choice (la • ter)

37. second choice (anything)

38. third choice (blue)

39. second choice (biggest)

40. second choice (soon)

41. third choice (house)

42. first choice (play)

43. second choice (wonder)

44. third choice (need)

45. first choice (bite)

46. second choice (nose)

47. third choice (teacher)

48. first choice (met)

49. second choice (more old)

50. third choice (book)

51. first choice (most)

Reading – Part 4: Writing Conventions

52. second choice (Max wants to eat dinner.)

53. third choice (saturday)

54. first choice (are)

55. first choice (smallest)

56. third choice (They take a walk.)

57. second choice (Mary isn't at home today.)

58. third choice (Bill saw her on the bus.)

59. first choice (fish)

60. second choice (walked)

Writing – Part 5

Prompt: Children are asked to write about something new they have learned to do this year and describe how it made them feel.

Scoring: Use one of the Narrative Writing Scoring Rubrics on pages T11–T12 to help you assess children's compositions. Choose one of the four rubrics, and assign each composition a score based on the 6-point, 5-point, 4-point, or 3-point scale.

OPTIONAL — FLUENCY CHECKS OR RUNNING RECORDS

How to Administer and Score a Fluency Test

A fluency test measures a child's reading rate, or the number of correctly read words per minute (wcpm), on grade-level text the child has not seen before. Give the child a copy of the Student Copy of the passage for the test and make a copy of the Teacher Copy for yourself, noting the formula for calculation at the bottom of the page. The Teacher Copy has a scale of running numbers to make it easier for you to know how many words the child read during the fluency check, while the passages in the student edition do not have the numbers. Make sure you have put the child's name and the test date at the top of your copy of the passage. Have a watch or clock available for timing the reading.

Have the child read the text aloud. Do not have the child read the title as part of the fluency reading; it is not included in the running word count. (You may want to tape-record the child's reading for later evaluation.) Stop the child at exactly one minute and note precisely where the child stopped.

As the child reads orally, on your copy of the text, mark any miscues or errors the child makes during the reading (see the chart on page T104). Count the total number of words the child read in one minute. Subtract any words the child read incorrectly. Record the words correct per minute score on the test.

The formula is: Total # of words read – # of errors = words correct per minute (wcpm).

How to Identify Reading Miscues/Errors

Using the passage on page T105, the chart below shows the kinds of miscues and errors to look for as a child reads aloud and the notations to use to mark them.

Reading Miscue	Notations
Omission The child omits words or word parts.	Some days are ⓢⓞcold!
Substitution The child substitutes words or parts of words for the words in the text.	Bears go to caves ~~to~~ *and* sleep.
Insertion The child inserts words or parts of words that are not in the text.	Small children like to run *out* in the cold. ∧
Mispronunciation/Misreading The child pronounces or reads a word incorrectly.	Cold winds *Came* come.
Hesitation The child hesitates over a word and the teacher provides the word.	*H* Children have mittens and hats so they can play outside.
Self-correction The child reads a word incorrectly but then corrects the error.	*sc* Big children like to skate on the ice.

Notes
- If the child hesitates over a word, wait several seconds before telling the child what the word is.

- If a child makes the same error more than once, count it as only one error.

- Self-correction is not counted as an actual error. However, writing "SC" over the word or words will help you identify words that give the child some difficulty.

Sample Fluency Test

Here is the passage marked as shown on the chart on the previous page. As the child reads the passage aloud to you, mark miscues and errors. Have the child read for exactly one minute, and then mark the last word the child reads.

Name _Susan_ _9/7/2011_

Wind and Ice

Some days are (so) cold! Cold winds ~~come~~ *came*. There is ice. | 11

Bears go to caves ~~to~~ *and* sleep. *H* Children have mittens and hats so | 23

they can play outside. Small children like to run ^*out* in the cold. | 35

Big children like to skate *(sc)* on the | ice. They all ride on sleds. | 48

They slide down the white hills. Cold days are fun! | 58

$$42 - 5 = 37$$

Interpreting the Results

According to one published norm for oral reading fluency, children at the end of a grade level should be reading fluently according to this chart.

End of Unit/Grade		Reading Rate (wcpm)
Grade 1	Unit R	N/A
Grade 1	Unit 1	N/A
Grade 1	Unit 2	N/A
Grade 1	Unit 3	25 to 35
Grade 1	Unit 4	35 to 45
Grade 1	Unit 5	45 to 60
End-of-Year Goal		60

If a child's reading rate is lower than the suggested progress toward the standard for his or her grade level, your notes on the child's miscues may help you determine why the rate is low. Does the child make errors that indicate his or her decoding skills are poor? If so, further instruction in phonics may be needed. Do the errors reflect a lack of comprehension or limited vocabulary? In that case, instruction in comprehension strategies and exposure to more vocabulary words may help. A lack of fluency may indicate a lack of exposure to models of fluent oral reading. It may also mean that the child isn't reading enough material at his or her reading level.

How to Take a Running Record

A Running Record is an assessment of oral reading accuracy and oral reading fluency. A child's reading accuracy is based on the number of words read correctly. This measure is determined by an analysis of the errors a child makes—a miscue analysis. Reading fluency is based on reading rate (the number of words read per minute) and the degree to which the child reads with a "natural flow."

A Running Record may be taken using any reading selection at any time. However, the most valid and reliable assessment fulfills these requirements: (1) the text is appropriate to the child's reading level and interest; (2) the text is unfamiliar to the child. The passages in this section are well-suited for use as either a Fluency Test or with a Running Record because they fit these requirements. For additional administrations that involve a Running Record, you may choose other passages from grade-level appropriate texts.

The Running Record may be used to verify instructional decisions suggested by other assessments, such as a Baseline Group or Benchmark Test. It may also be used to identify a child's particular strengths and weaknesses in reading and language development. In addition, the Running Record may be administered periodically throughout the year as a means of monitoring a child's progress.

Measuring oral reading accuracy and oral reading fluency may be accomplished in a single reading, but two different operations are required. The guidelines on pages T107–T108 explain how to determine each measurement.

How to Measure Oral Reading Accuracy

1. Choose an appropriate grade-level text of about 100 to 200 words, or use those passages that have been provided for use as a Fluency Test.

2. Make copies of the text—one (of the Student Copy) for the child and one (of the Teacher Copy) for you. If the text appears in a book, you may have the child read the text from the book.

3. Give the text to the child and have the child read the text aloud. (You may want to tape-record the child's reading for later evaluation. This approach can be especially helpful if you are timing the child's reading or conducting other assessments at the same time.)

4. On your copy of the text, mark any miscues or errors the child makes during the reading (see the explanation of reading miscues/errors listed for Fluency Tests).

5. Count the total number of errors the child makes and find the percentage score for the number of errors. If you are using a passage from this book of Fluency/ Running Record Passages, the total word count is indicated for each passage and a formula for determining a percentage score is provided.

6. If you are using a text from a different source, use this formula to get a percentage score:

$$\frac{\text{Total \# of words minus \# of errors}}{\text{Total \# of words}} \times 100 = \text{percentage score}$$

Example: Suppose a child reads a text of 110 words and makes 6 errors.

$$\frac{110 - 6 = 104 \text{ words}}{110} = 0.945 \qquad 0.945 \times 100 = 94.5\% \text{ (round to 95\%)}$$

The percentage score indicates the child's oral reading accuracy (percentage of words in the passage read correctly).

How to Measure Reading Rate

Reading rate is generally defined as number of words per minute (wpm). To determine the reading rate, follow steps 1–3 as described on page T107. Note the exact time when the child begins reading and the time when he or she finishes.

To calculate the number of words per minute, use the formula below:

$$\frac{\text{Total \# of words read}}{\text{\# of seconds}} \times 60 = \text{words per minute}$$

Example: Suppose a child reads a passage of 120 words in 90 seconds.

$$\frac{120}{90} = 1.33 \text{ (round to the nearest hundredth)}$$

$1.33 \times 60 = 79.8$ words per minute (round to 80 wpm)

Interpreting the Results

For oral reading accuracy, use the following criteria:

- A child who reads 98%–100% of the words correctly is reading at an independent level and may need more challenging texts.

- A child who reads 91%–97% of the words correctly is reading at an instructional level and will likely benefit from guided instruction in the regular program.

- A child who reads with an accuracy of 90% or less is reading at a frustration level and may benefit most from targeted instruction with lower-level texts or intervention.

For any child whose Running Record results are not clearly definitive, we recommend administering additional individual assessments, such as classroom observations and anecdotal records. For more information about other assessments, refer to the *Assessment Handbook*.

On the following pages you will find passages that may be used for either fluency or running record tests. Both a Teacher Copy and a Student Copy have been provided.

Student Name _____ Date _____

Walks in the Park

I like to go walking in the park. Dad and I always see other people. They are	17
walking or running. They ride their bikes around the edge of the park. Some of	32
them stop. They talk to us. We meet new people. Then I get to shake hands.	48
We see squirrels in the trees. We see ducks by the water too. Dad does not let	65
me chase them. I still have fun.	72

Fluency Test

☐ – ☐ = ☐ (wcpm)

Running Record

Oral Reading Accuracy: Reading Rate:

$$\frac{\boxed{} - \boxed{}}{\boxed{}} \times 100 = \boxed{\%}$$ $$\frac{\boxed{}}{\boxed{}} \times 60 = \boxed{} \text{ (wpm)}$$

Walks in the Park

I like to go walking in the park. Dad and I always see other people. They are walking or running. They ride their bikes around the edge of the park. Some of them stop. They talk to us. We meet new people. Then I get to shake hands.

We see squirrels in the trees. We see ducks by the water too. Dad does not let me chase them. I still have fun.

Student Name _____ Date _____

Annie and Her Friends

    Annie is a little dog. She has very short legs. She does not have a tail. Annie | 17

plays with Peek, Boo, and Bo. They have long legs. They have tails too. | 31

    Peek is Annie's best friend. Once Annie gave Peek some old socks as a present. | 46

Peek takes a sock when she must ride in the car. It makes her feel better. | 62

    Annie likes to chase her ball. Peek likes to chew on her toy frog. Boo and Bo | 79

like to eat. When the dogs play together, they all like to bark. | 92

Fluency Test

☐ – ☐ = ☐ (wcpm)

Running Record

Oral Reading Accuracy: Reading Rate:

$$\frac{\boxed{} - \boxed{}}{\boxed{}} \times 100 = \boxed{} \%$$

$$\frac{\boxed{}}{\boxed{}} \times 60 = \boxed{} \text{ (wpm)}$$

Annie and Her Friends

Annie is a little dog. She has very short legs. She does not have a tail. Annie plays with Peek, Boo, and Bo. They have long legs. They have tails too.

Peek is Annie's best friend. Once Annie gave Peek some old socks as a present. Peek takes a sock when she must ride in the car. It makes her feel better.

Annie likes to chase her ball. Peek likes to chew on her toy frog. Boo and Bo like to eat. When the dogs play together, they all like to bark.

Student Name _____ Date _____

The House in the Woods

My family lives in a house in the woods. We look out the windows and see tall	17
trees all around us.	21
We see birds in many bright colors. The birds are red or blue or yellow. We see	38
some little brown ones too. We give seeds to them. They visit us and eat a snack.	55
We see different animals. Many squirrels live in the trees. Some of them are red.	70
Others are gray. They all like to eat nuts. Rabbits and foxes live in the woods too.	87
What do we like best? We like watching the deer.	97
We cannot see other people or houses. Our friends and neighbors are the birds	111
and animals that live in the woods with us.	120

Fluency Test

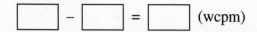

□ − □ = □ (wcpm)

Running Record

Oral Reading Accuracy:　　　　　　　　　　Reading Rate:

$$\frac{\boxed{} - \boxed{}}{\boxed{}} \times 100 = \boxed{} \% \qquad \frac{\boxed{}}{\boxed{}} \times 60 = \boxed{} \text{ (wpm)}$$

The House in the Woods

My family lives in a house in the woods. We look out the windows and see tall trees all around us.

We see birds in many bright colors. The birds are red or blue or yellow. We see some little brown ones too. We give seeds to them. They visit us and eat a snack.

We see different animals. Many squirrels live in the trees. Some of them are red. Others are gray. They all like to eat nuts. Rabbits and foxes live in the woods too. What do we like best? We like watching the deer.

We cannot see other people or houses. Our friends and neighbors are the birds and animals that live in the woods with us.

NAME _____   DATE _____

Scott Foresman
Benchmark Test
Unit R
My World

Grade 1

Glenview, Illinois
Boston, Massachusetts
Chandler, Arizona
Upper Saddle River, New Jersey

ISBN-13: 978-0-328-53723-5
ISBN-10:   0-328-53723-3

1 2 3 4 5 6 7 8 9 10 V016 19 18 17 16 15 14 13 12 11 10
CC1

ISBN-13: 978-0-328-53723-5
ISBN-10:   0-328-53723-3

PHONEMIC AWARENESS

GO ON

Benchmark Test   Unit R

PHONEMIC AWARENESS

GO ON

PHONEMIC AWARENESS

Benchmark Test   Unit R

PHONICS

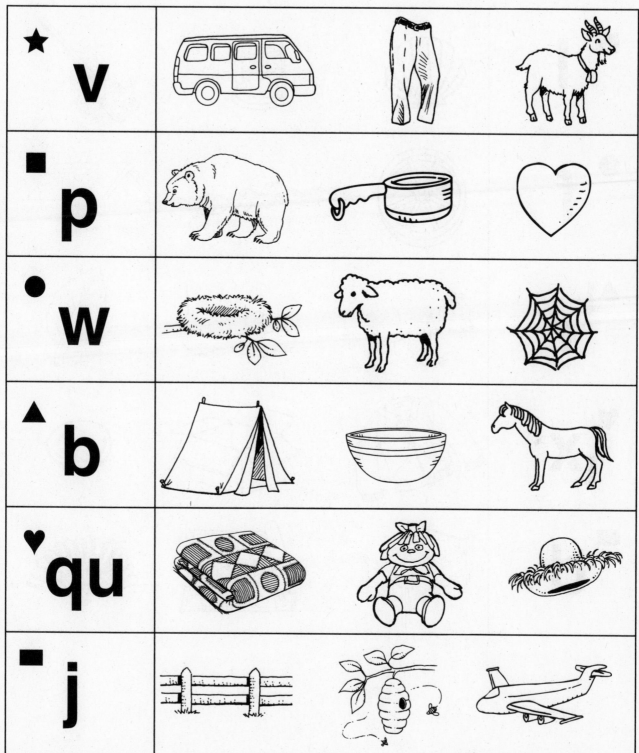

★ v

■ p

● w

▲ b

♥ qu

▬ j

GO ON

PHONICS

Benchmark Test   Unit R

WORD READING

★	hat	fan	hen
■	tub	big	bus
●	lip	leg	jug
▲	den	desk	bed
♥	pen	pat	bend
■	net	mud	pet

GO ON

WORD READING

■	mop	log	mug
●	car	cup	can
▲	ham	land	lamp
♥	web	wet	red
■	gift	tent	girl

WORD KNOWLEDGE

■	the	three	he
●	look	you	yellow
▲	was	is	he
♥	like	look	have
■	where	green	here

WORD KNOWLEDGE

■	to	you	look
●	that	they	three
▲	for	to	are
♥	the	you	with
▬	three	we	have

COMPREHENSION

GO ON

COMPREHENSION

Benchmark Test   Unit R

WRITING

NAME _____ DATE _____

Scott Foresman
Benchmark Test
Unit 1
Animals, Tame and Wild

PEARSON

Glenview, Illinois
Boston, Massachusetts
Chandler, Arizona
Upper Saddle River, New Jersey

ISBN-13: 978-0-328-53724-2
ISBN-10:   0-328-53724-1

1 2 3 4 5 6 7 8 9 10 V016 19 18 17 16 15 14 13 12 11 10
CC1

ISBN-13: 978-0-328-53724-2
ISBN-10:   0-328-53724-1

EAN

9 780328 537242

90000>

PART 1: COMPREHENSION

Directions
Read about how Ox tries to help Bird. Then answer Numbers 1 through 14.

Ox and Bird

Ox plays on the rocks.
Bird is up in the tree.
Bird sees Ox playing.

Ox looks up in the tree.
Ox sees Bird.

GO ON

 Bird, come sit on a rock with me.

 I must sit on my nest. I can not play.

 Can I help you?

 Ox, you are TOO BIG! Go home.

1

2

3

4

She did not like Ox.

She had to sit on the nest.

She did not like rocks.

5

 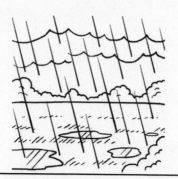 

6

A bird had a nest.

An ox was on the rocks.

A bird said to go home.

7

8

on the rocks

on a nest

in a tree

GO ON

9 He is too big.

He wants to play.

He likes the rocks.

---

10 Ox and Bird Play

Bird on the Rocks

Ox Can Not Help

---

11 help Bird

eat Bird

go home

12

13

14

Ox saw Bird.

Bird said to go home.

Ox was on the rocks.

PART 2: HIGH-FREQUENCY WORDS

15 help   them   her

---

16 eat   this   tree

---

17 from   use   up

---

18 your   home   many

---

19 too   take   on

---

20 get   saw   way

PART 3: PHONICS

21   tip   tap   top

---

22   sack   sick   sock

---

23   fox   hot   six

---

24   nut   hot   let

---

25   kicks   locks   racks

GO ON

26   tree   rocks   nest

---

27   playing   play   plays

---

28   dog   dug   dig

---

29   plan   glad   land

---

30   rub   rip   rob

31   hen   rust   rat

32   sees   seeing   see

33   step   not   best

34   pot   pit   pet

PART 4: WRITING CONVENTIONS

35   She sees the trees.

Sees the trees.

The trees.

---

36   is

green

The tree

---

37   runs

She

home

---

38   Sits on the nest the bird.

The bird sits on the nest.

The nest the bird sits on.

39   I like to play in the park.

Do you like to play in the park?

Playing in the park.

---

40   They watch the zebras play.

The zebras play.

Where do the zebras play?

PART 5: WRITING

NAME _____ DATE _____

Scott Foresman
Benchmark Test
Unit 2
Communities

Glenview, Illinois
Boston, Massachusetts
Chandler, Arizona
Upper Saddle River, New Jersey

ISBN-13: 978-0-328-53725-9
ISBN-10:   0-328-53725-X
1 2 3 4 5 6 7 8 9 10 V016 19 18 17 16 15 14 13 12 11 10
CC1

ISBN-13: 978-0-328-53725-9
ISBN-10:   0-328-53725-X
EAN
9 780328 537259
90000>

PART 1: COMPREHENSION

Directions
Little Bear wants dinner. Read the story to find out how Big Bear finds it. Then answer Numbers 1 through 14.

Finding Dinner

Little Bear needed dinner.
There was no food!
Big Bear said, "I'll go out.
I have a place to chase animals."

Big Bear walked around the huge forest.

He wanted to catch mice.

He couldn't find them.

He came to a nice lake.

He hunted for fish.

He just got wet feet.

He was sad.

Then he looked for honey.
It was in the tall trees!

Big Bear ran home.
He gave the honey to Little Bear.
Little Bear ate it all!
"Thank you, Big Bear," said Little Bear.

1 **What gave Big Bear wet feet?**

○ walking in the forest

○ hunting in the water

○ looking in the trees

2 **What is this story all about?**

○ helping

○ walking

○ playing

3 **What made Big Bear sad?**

○ He did not like the mice.

○ He could not get honey.

○ He could not find food.

4 **Big Bear got some honey. Then he went**

○ to the lake.

○ to the forest.

○ back home.

5 The author wrote the story to tell about

○ two bears.

○ all animals.

○ mice and fish.

6 What is a good name for this story?

○ Big Bear Has Fun

○ Big Bear Helps Little Bear

○ Little Bear Is Sad

7 When there was no food, Big Bear had to

○ get dinner.

○ go out to play.

○ get help.

8 What did Big Bear want to do?

○ grow food

○ play

○ find food

9 The author wanted
- ○ to make you safe in the forest.
- ○ you to see Big Bear helping Little Bear.
- ○ to tell you where to find honey.

10 How can you tell this story is make-believe?
- ○ Big Bear could talk.
- ○ Big Bear looked for food.
- ○ Little Bear liked honey.

11 Where did Big Bear look for food last?
- ○ in the lake
- ○ in the trees
- ○ in the park

12 At the end of the story, the author wanted you to
- ○ eat your dinner.
- ○ be sad.
- ○ feel good.

13 Where did this story take place?

○ in a forest

○ in a lake

○ in a town

14 At the end of the story, Little Bear was

○ sad.

○ glad.

○ mad.

PART 2: HIGH-FREQUENCY WORDS

Directions

For Numbers 15 through 20, find the word that fits best in each sentence.

15 The dog can not _____ his bone.
- ○ family
- ○ some
- ○ find

16 It was cold. We _____ not go to the zoo.
- ○ could
- ○ new
- ○ put

17 Jane put seeds in the cage. The birds needed _____.
- ○ good
- ○ food
- ○ grow

18 We all rode bikes _____ the big park.
- ○ also
- ○ around
- ○ people

10

19 We wanted to go _____, but Mom said to play inside.

- ○ out
- ○ under
- ○ horse

20 Is _____ a place you will let us play?

- ○ now
- ○ old
- ○ there

PART 3: PHONICS

Directions
For Numbers 21 through 34, listen to the question and fill in the circle under the correct answer.

21
mice   wish   lost
○   ○   ○

22
talked   made   wanted
○   ○   ○

23
two   tree   they
○   ○   ○

24
made   need   man
○   ○   ○

25

nose	nest	nice
○	○	○

26

dash	rice	was
○	○	○

27

can	shine	chin
○	○	○

28

page	pig	tug
○	○	○

29

wish	witch	with
○	○	○

GO ON

30

I do   I am   I will

○   ○   ○

31

third   top   tall

○   ○   ○

32

wet   bee   go

○   ○   ○

33

bone   box   hot

○   ○   ○

34

picnic   kite   snack

○   ○   ○

PART 4: WRITING CONVENTIONS

Directions
For Numbers 35 through 40, find the one that is the best.

35 The _____ is in the water.

○ could

○ under

○ fish

36 There are four _____ in the park.

○ workers

○ worker

○ work

37 ○ My cat tom plays with mice.

○ My cat Tom plays with mice.

○ My Cat tom plays with mice.

GO ON

38

○ I like Mrs. Jones.

○ I like Mrs. jones.

○ I like mrs. jones.

39

○ We play ball on sunday.

○ We play Ball on sunday.

○ We play ball on Sunday.

40

○ It is hot in june.

○ It is hot in June.

○ It is Hot in June.

Benchmark Test   Unit 2

PROMPT

In "Finding Dinner," Little Bear wants to eat.
Is there a sandwich that you like to eat best?
How do you make this sandwich?
Draw a picture of the sandwich you like to
eat best.
Then write to tell how to make the sandwich.

CHECKLIST FOR WRITERS

_____ Did I think about how to make the sandwich before I
started writing?

_____ Did I tell what steps to take to make it?

_____ Did I put the steps in the right order?

_____ Do my sentences make sense?

_____ Do my sentences begin with capital letters?

_____ Do my sentences end with end marks?

_____ Did I check my spelling?

_____ Did I make sure my paper is the way I want readers to read it?

PART 5: WRITING

Scott Foresman
Benchmark Test
Unit 3
Changes

Glenview, Illinois
Boston, Massachusetts
Chandler, Arizona
Upper Saddle River, New Jersey

ISBN-13: 978-0-328-53726-6
ISBN-10:   0-328-53726-8
1 2 3 4 5 6 7 8 9 10 V016 19 18 17 16 15 14 13 12 11 10
CC1

ISBN-13: 978-0-328-53726-6
ISBN-10:   0-328-53726-8

EAN

9 780328 537266

90000>

PART 1: COMPREHENSION

Directions
Many things start to happen in spring. Read about them. Then answer Numbers 1 through 7.

Is It Spring?

Raccoon looked out from the tree.
"Is it spring?" he asked.
"It isn't cold any more," said Bird.

"The rain has stopped," said Caterpillar.
"The flowers are growing again."
"Then I think it's spring!" shouted Raccoon.
He ran down the tree.
He went running to see his friends.

GO ON

Bird flew away.

The sun did feel warmer on her feathers.

She went looking for a good place to make a nest.

Caterpillar crawled around the tree.
It was time to eat dinner.
The leaves were very green.
He eats the greenest ones.
Soon he will be fat.
Then he will become a beautiful butterfly.

GO ON

1 **What did Bird do at the end of the story?**

○ She flew to see Raccoon.

○ She looked for a place for a nest.

○ She crawled around the tree.

2 **How are Raccoon, Bird, and Caterpillar the same?**

○ They are all happy it is spring.

○ They all want to see their friends.

○ They all need to eat leaves.

3 **How are Bird and Caterpillar different?**

○ Bird needs to eat leaves.

○ Bird likes the spring.

○ Bird needs to make a nest.

4 **What did Raccoon do first?**

○ He ate leaves from the tree.

○ He looked out from the tree.

○ He ran to the ground.

5 **How did the animals know it was spring?**

○ The grass was green.

○ It was raining.

○ They saw flowers.

6 How can you tell this story is make-believe?

   ○ The animals talked.

   ○ Raccoon ran down the tree.

   ○ Caterpillar turned into a butterfly.

7 In this story, the author wanted to

   ○ make you feel sad about spring.

   ○ make you plant flowers in spring.

   ○ tell you what animals do in the spring.

Directions

Write your answer to Question A on the lines below. Base your answer on the story "Is It Spring?"

A   Do you like spring? Tell why or why not.

_____

- -

_____

_____

- -

_____

_____

- -

_____

_____

- -

_____

_____

- -

_____

_____

- -

_____

Directions

Moving to a new house can be hard. Read about Dan. Then answer Numbers 8 through 14.

New Friends

Dan had moved to a new house.

He watched from inside.

The workers were bringing in the boxes with his things.

Dan did not want to be in a new house.

He did not want to go to a new school.

GO ON

Dan saw some kids playing in the park.

His mother saw them too.

She said, "Dan, do you want to go to the park and play?"

Dan went to the park.
He played with his new friends.
His new friend Bill said, "We've had fun.
We'll help you on your first day of school."

GO ON

When Dan came home, he had a smile on his face.

8 **How did this story start?**

    ○ Dan made a new friend.

    ○ Dan came to a new house.

    ○ Dan went to a new school.

9 **What did Dan do first?**

    ○ He went to school.

    ○ He played in the park.

    ○ He watched the workers.

10 **Why did Dan smile at the end?**

    ○ He was glad to have a new friend.

    ○ He had many things to play with.

    ○ He saw some of his old friends.

11 **The big idea of this story is**

    ○ playing in the park.

    ○ talking with Mother.

    ○ finding new friends.

12 **What did Dan do last?**

    ○ He came home.

    ○ He talked to his mother.

    ○ He went to school.

GO ON

13 At the end of this story

○ Dan wanted to move away.

○ Dan was happy he had friends.

○ Dan did not like his new house.

14 How did Dan change in this story?

○ First he was sad, and then he was happy.

○ First he was mad, and then he was sad.

○ First he was happy, and then he was sad.

Directions

Write your answer to Question B on the lines below. Base your answer on the two stories you have read.

B In the story "Is It Spring?" you met Raccoon. In the story "New Friends" you met Dan. How are Dan and Raccoon alike?

WRITING ACROSS TEXTS

_____

- -

_____

- -

_____

- -

_____

- -

_____

- -

_____

- -

_____

- -

_____

PART 2: HIGH-FREQUENCY WORDS

Directions

For Numbers 15 through 20, find the word that best fits in each sentence.

15 Mark takes the bus to _____.

- ○ were
- ○ stay
- ○ school

16 His family lives in a big _____.

- ○ enough
- ○ house
- ○ our

17 My grandmother lives far _____.

- ○ away
- ○ any
- ○ afraid

18 "Your hands are still dirty," said Dad. "You must wash them _____."

- ○ again
- ○ wait
- ○ push

19 I did not eat any lunch. I hope Mother has dinner for us
_____.

- ○ how
- ○ soon
- ○ know

20 There is no rain. This is a good _____ to play outside.

- ○ any
- ○ done
- ○ day

PART 3: PHONICS

Directions

For Numbers 21 through 34, fill in the circle under the correct answer.

21 It was time to eat dinner.
Which word has the same sound as the i in time?

    wig   bee   why

    ○   ○   ○

22 The leaves were very green.
Which word has the same ending sound as very?

    fly   penny   try

    ○   ○   ○

23 Soon he will be fat.
Which word rhymes with he?

    tree   cute   her

    ○   ○   ○

24 Then he will become a beautiful butterfly.
Which word is made of two words put together?

    will   butterfly   beautiful

    ○   ○   ○

25 It is <u>spring</u>.
Which word has the same ending sound as <u>spring</u>?

wag ○   wink ○   wing ○

26 Mother tells Dan to <u>go</u> to the park.
Which word rhymes with <u>go</u>?

no ○   for ○   to ○

27 The workers bring in <u>boxes</u>.
Which word has the same sound as the <u>es</u> in <u>boxes</u>?

trees ○   cakes ○   dishes ○

28 Raccoon said

Then I <u>think</u> it's spring.

Which word has the same ending sound as <u>think</u>?

then ○   bank ○   thing ○

29 Bird said

It isn't cold any <u>more</u>.

Which word rhymes with <u>more</u>?

store ○   star ○   fur ○

GO ON

30 The animals know <u>it's</u> spring.
<u>It's</u> means

it was. ○

it is. ○

it will. ○

31 Caterpillar eats the <u>greenest</u> leaves.
The <u>greenest</u> leaves are

the most green. ○

not green. ○

a little green. ○

32 Dan plays in the <u>park</u>.
Which word has the same middle sound as <u>park</u>?

dirt ○

pack ○

dart ○

33 Caterpillar sees that it is not raining any more.
The rain has

stoped. ○

stopped. ○

stopt. ○

34 Bill said

We've had fun.

What two words make up <u>we've</u>?

we are ○

we will ○

we have ○

PART 4: WRITING CONVENTIONS

Directions
Fill in the circle for your answers for Numbers 35 through 40.

35 **Which word is a verb?**

○ eat

○ always

○ old

36 He _____ the horse.

○ rided

○ ride

○ rides

37 They _____ to go to the park.

○ wants

○ wanting

○ want

38 **Which one tells what is happening now?**

○ She looks at the ground.

○ She looked at the ground.

○ She was looking at the ground.

GO ON

39 Which one tells what happened in the past?

- ○ We walk to school.
- ○ We walked to school.
- ○ We are walking to school.

40 Which sentence is written correctly?

- ○ They wont' come inside.
- ○ They wo'nt come inside.
- ○ They won't come inside.

PART 5: WRITING

PROMPT

In "Is It Spring?" the animals see flowers growing. Think of what it's like outside in the spring. Write to tell what spring is like.

CHECKLIST FOR WRITERS

_____ Did I think about spring before I started to write?

_____ Did I tell what spring is like?

_____ Did I use sense words to tell about things I can see, hear, smell, taste, or touch in the spring?

_____ Do my sentences make sense?

_____ Do my sentences begin with capital letters?

_____ Do my sentences end with end marks?

_____ Did I check my spelling?

_____ Did I make sure my paper is the way I want readers to read it?

NAME _____ DATE _____

Scott Foresman
Benchmark Test
Unit 4
Treasures

Reading STREET
Grade 1

PEARSON

Glenview, Illinois
Boston, Massachusetts
Chandler, Arizona
Upper Saddle River, New Jersey

ISBN-13: 978-0-328-53727-3
ISBN-10:   0-328-53727-6

1 2 3 4 5 6 7 8 9 10 V016 19 18 17 16 15 14 13 12 11 10
CC1

ISBN-13: 978-0-328-53727-3
ISBN-10:   0-328-53727-6

Directions

Sometimes friends must say good-bye. Read this story about two friends. Then answer Numbers 1 through 7.

A Wonderful Friend

Lee and Pam are good friends. They go to the same school. They enjoy math together. They like to draw and read. Lee and Pam play in the park every day after school.

Pam's mother takes care of birds. She helps them grow. She shows their feathers to Lee and Pam.

GO ON

One day Pam's mother finds a new job. Pam and her family must go away.

Pam worries. Will she ever see Lee again?

Lee gives Pam a present.

"What is it?" asks Pam. She opens the present.

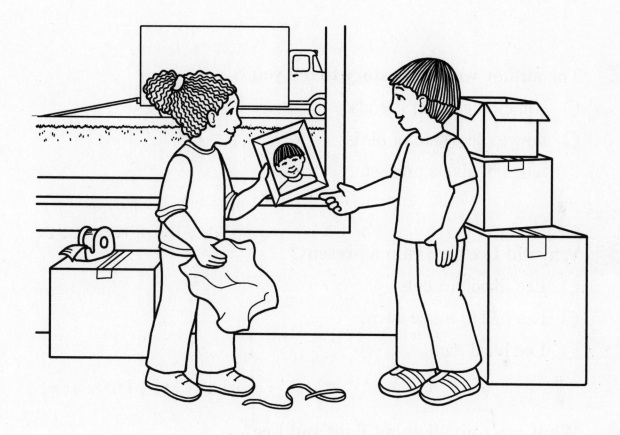

"Surprise!" yells Lee. "It's a picture of me!"

"How nice," sighs Pam. "Good-bye. Be sure to write!"

"Good-bye." Lee waves to Pam. "I will write soon."

Pam feels happy. Lee will always be her wonderful friend.

GO ON

1 **Why did Pam's family have to go away?**

  ○ Pam's mother had a new job.

  ○ Pam's mother cared for birds.

  ○ Lee's mother had a new job.

2 **The author wrote this story to tell you**

  ○ something about friends.

  ○ how to take care of birds.

  ○ when to give a present.

3 **Why did Lee give Pam a present?**

  ○ Lee liked presents.

  ○ Lee had to move away.

  ○ Lee liked Pam.

4 **What can you tell about Pam and Lee?**

  ○ They helped birds grow.

  ○ They liked to be together.

  ○ They did not like school.

5 **What does this story teach us?**

  ○ It is hard to find a job.

  ○ It is fun to move away.

  ○ It is good to have friends.

6 What can you tell about Pam's mother?

 ○ She did not want to move.

 ○ She liked birds.

 ○ She liked surprises.

7 What happened at the end of this story?

 ○ Lee and Pam said good-bye.

 ○ Pam's mother showed feathers to Lee.

 ○ Lee went to play in the park.

Directions

Write your answer to Question A on the lines below. Base your answer on "A Wonderful Friend."

A   In "A Wonderful Friend," Lee's friend Pam has to move away. Tell how you would feel if a good friend had to move away. Tell what present you would give your friend.

_____

- -

_____

- -

_____

- -

_____

- -

_____

- -

_____

- -

_____

- -

_____

- -

_____

- -

Read about how to help a hurt hummingbird. Then answer Numbers 8 through 14.

How to Be a Hummingbird's Friend

Hummingbirds are very small birds. They are beautiful. They have shiny red and blue feathers. Their homes are nests.

Hummingbirds enjoy flying. You may see hummingbirds near flowers. They drink nectar from the flowers. This is their food.

GO ON

Hummingbirds can get hurt. If you find one, do not worry. You can try to help it.

Pick up the hummingbird slowly. It may be afraid. It is a wild animal. It does not know you are its friend.

Place the hummingbird in a box to keep it warm. Feed the hummingbird water mixed with nectar. You cannot do anything more to help it.

If the hummingbird gets better, you must say good-bye. Let it go. Watch it fly away. It is good that you were the hummingbird's friend.

8 What should you do first if you find a hurt hummingbird?

○ Pick it up slowly.

○ Let it fly home.

○ Feed it water mixed with nectar.

9 What does this story teach us about?

○ flying

○ eating

○ helping

10 Which of these statements is an opinion?

○ Hummingbirds are very small birds.

○ Hummingbirds are beautiful.

○ The homes of hummingbirds are nests.

11 The author wrote "How to Be a Hummingbird's Friend" to tell

○ why hummingbirds are beautiful.

○ where to find hummingbirds.

○ how to take care of a hurt hummingbird.

GO ON

12 A hummingbird might be afraid of you because

○ it is a wild animal.

○ it has shiny red and blue feathers.

○ it gets its food from flowers.

13 How can you keep a hummingbird warm?

○ Give it water mixed with nectar.

○ Place it in a box.

○ Let it fly away when it is better.

14 Which of these statements is an opinion?

○ It is good that you were the hummingbird's friend.

○ Pick up the hummingbird slowly.

○ Nectar is the food of hummingbirds.

Directions

Write your answer to Question B on the lines below. Base your answer on the two stories you have read.

B Both "A Wonderful Friend" and "How to Be a Hummingbird's Friend" are about friends. How are the friends in these stories different?

WRITING ACROSS TEXTS

_____

_____

_____

_____

_____

_____

_____

_____

_____

_____

_____

_____

_____

_____

PART 2: HIGH-FREQUENCY WORDS

Directions
Fill in the circle beside your answer choice for Numbers 15 through 20.

15 Tim liked art. He _____ beautiful pictures.

○ dance

○ drew

○ about

16 "Your dance will be great," said Father. "Don't _____ at all."

○ worry

○ enough

○ took

17 The girls like games. They _____ playing Go Fish.

○ across

○ because

○ enjoy

18 We had a gift for Mom. It was a _____.

○ stood

○ surprise

○ remember

19 A hummingbird is not a pet. It is a _____ animal.

○ wild

○ would

○ told

20 "Is that a new book?" asked Dad. "Will you _____ it to me?"

○ touch

○ found

○ show

PART 3: PHONICS

Directions

For Numbers 21 through 34, fill in the circle under the correct answer.

21 Lee and Pam <u>play</u> in the park.
Which word rhymes with <u>play</u>?

    stay   back   math
    ○   ○   ○

22 Pam's mother helps birds <u>grow</u>.
Which word has the same sound as the <u>ow</u> in <u>grow</u>?

    job   soon   boat
    ○   ○   ○

23 Lee and Pam like to draw and <u>read</u>.
Which word has the same sound as the <u>ea</u> in <u>read</u>?

    train   meat   sled
    ○   ○   ○

24 Pam <u>sighs</u> when she gets a present.
Which word has the same sound as the <u>igh</u> in <u>sighs</u>?

    ride   lift   pig
    ○   ○   ○

25 Lee said

I will write to you <u>soon</u>.

Which word has the same sound as the <u>oo</u> in <u>soon</u>?

coat   show   fruit
○   ○   ○

26 Pam said

Be <u>sure</u> to <u>write</u>.

Which word has the same beginning sound as <u>write</u>?

when   wait   room
○   ○   ○

27 Find the word that is best in the sentence.

_____ **mother has a new job.**

Pam   Pam's   Pams
○   ○   ○

28 **Hummingbirds are <u>beautiful</u>.**
The word <u>beautiful</u> means

has no beauty.   wants beauty.   full of beauty.
○   ○   ○

29 **They have shiny red and <u>blue</u> feathers.**
Which word rhymes with <u>blue</u>?

flew   fly   blow
○   ○   ○

GO ON

30 A hummingbird does not <u>know</u> you are its friend.
Which word has the same beginning sound as <u>know</u>?

need ○   kick ○   kite ○

31 You cannot do anything more to help it.
Which word is a compound word?

anything ○   more ○   help ○

32 Hummingbirds have beautiful <u>feathers</u>.
Which word has the same sound as the <u>ea</u> in <u>feathers</u>?

sea ○   food ○   bread ○

33 The hummingbird may be <u>afraid</u>.
Which word has the same sound as the <u>ai</u> in <u>afraid</u>?

map ○   like ○   made ○

34 Pick up the hummingbird <u>slowly</u>.
What means the same as <u>slowly</u>?

○ in a quick way
○ in a slow way
○ in an easy way

PART 4: WRITING CONVENTIONS

Directions
Fill in the circle for your answer choice for Numbers 35 through 40.

35 Which word in this sentence tells about the bird's feathers?
The bird has green feathers.

- ○ bird
- ○ has
- ○ green

36 Which word in this sentence tells about the tree?
The pretty bird flew quickly to the big tree.

- ○ pretty
- ○ quickly
- ○ big

37 Which word in this sentence tells how many girls?
Nine little girls play under the tall tree.

- ○ nine
- ○ little
- ○ tall

GO ON

38 Which word in this sentence is a describing word?
The friends sang their sad song.

- ○ friends
- ○ sang
- ○ sad

Find the word that best fits in each sentence.

39 The baby is the _____ one in their family.

- ○ smallest
- ○ smaller
- ○ biggest

40 The boy is _____ than the hummingbird.

- ○ bigger
- ○ smallest
- ○ warmest

PART 5: WRITING

PROMPT

Pretend your good friend went to live in a new town. You would like to see your friend again. Write a letter to your friend. Ask your friend to come visit you.

Tell your friend all the good reasons to come for a visit. Write at least three sentences.

CHECKLIST FOR WRITERS

_____ Did I pretend that a good friend went to live in a new town?

_____ Did I ask my friend to come visit me?

_____ Did I tell why my friend should visit me?

_____ Did I write at least three sentences?

_____ Did I sign my letter?

_____ Do my sentences make sense?

_____ Do my sentences begin with capital letters?

_____ Do my sentences end with end marks?

_____ Did I check my spelling?

_____ Did I make sure my letter is the way I want readers to read it?

NAME _____ DATE _____

Scott Foresman
Benchmark Test

Unit 5
Great Ideas

Glenview, Illinois
Boston, Massachusetts
Chandler, Arizona
Upper Saddle River, New Jersey

ISBN-13: 978-0-328-53728-0
ISBN-10:   0-328-53728-4
1 2 3 4 5 6 7 8 9 10 V016 19 18 17 16 15 14 13 12 11 10
CC1

ISBN-13: 978-0-328-53728-0
ISBN-10:   0-328-53728-4

EAN

PART 1: COMPREHENSION

Directions
Two friends can make a rainy day fun. Learn what Dan and Joy do while it is raining. Then answer Numbers 1 through 7.

A Rainy Day

Dan said to his friend Joy, "I'm unhappy. I want to go outside. But it's raining. What should we do today?"

"I have an idea," said Joy. "Do you know how to draw?"

"Oh, yes," said Dan. "That's a good idea. We can do that!"

"I have always loved drawing," said Joy. "I want to try new things. I will use many colors and make beautiful pictures!"

All through the day Joy and Dan stayed inside. They used colored pens and paper. They drew birds and many other animals. They drew crocodiles, elephants, and hippos!

GO ON

"Joy, what is your favorite animal?" asked Dan.

"I like zebras," answered Joy.

Dan said, "I'll draw a herd of wild zebras for you."

Joy blinked her eyes and laughed. "One is enough!"

Joy and Dan didn't worry about the rain at all.

"Joy, you had a great idea," said Dan. "Rainy days can be fun!"

1 **Where did Joy and Dan spend the day?**
- ○ at the zoo
- ○ outside
- ○ inside

2 **What is the big idea in this story?**
- ○ Friends can always have a good time together.
- ○ There are many different kinds of animals.
- ○ It is easy to draw animals.

3 **Why was Dan sad at the beginning of the story?**
- ○ He did not know how to draw.
- ○ He did not want to be inside.
- ○ He did not want to play with Joy.

4 **What does this story teach us?**
- ○ how to draw pictures
- ○ why it rains
- ○ how to have fun

5 **How did "A Rainy Day" begin?**
- ○ Dan and Joy used paper and pens.
- ○ Dan and Joy saw that it was raining.
- ○ Dan and Joy drew zebras and birds.

GO ON

6 **What is "A Rainy Day" mostly about?**

○ two friends

○ wild zebras

○ a favorite animal

7 **What best tells about Joy?**

○ She wanted to draw more pictures than Dan.

○ She was tired of spending time with Dan.

○ She could have fun even on a rainy day.

Directions

Write your answer to Question A on the lines below. Base your answer on the story "A Rainy Day."

A   **What do you like to do on a rainy day? Tell three things you do.**

_____

- -

_____

- -

_____

- -

_____

- -

_____

- -

_____

- -

_____

- -

Directions

Have you ever wondered what a farmer does? Read "A Farmer's Life" and find out. Then answer Numbers 8 through 14.

A Farmer's Life

Farmers work hard. They give people many different kinds of food. Some farmers grow crops. Other farmers raise animals.

One crop that farmers grow is oats. Farmers feed oats to their animals. People eat oats too. They cook oatmeal and enjoy eating it with milk on top.

Another crop that farmers grow is corn. There are two kinds of corn. Farm animals eat one kind. The other kind is called sweet corn. People eat sweet corn.

GO ON

Some farmers raise animals such as cows. Cows give people milk. People also get meat from cattle. Pigs, sheep, and goats also live on some farms.

Farmers must get up early in the morning to do their work. They spend most of their time outside among their crops and animals. They almost never work inside. If you think being outside and working hard is fun, you might be a good farmer.

GO ON

8 **What is one kind of crop that farmers grow?**

○ goats

○ pigs

○ oats

9 **How are oats different from corn?**

○ They are used to feed animals.

○ They are made into oatmeal.

○ They are grown on farms.

10 **The author wrote "A Farmer's Life" to**

○ teach real things.

○ make you laugh.

○ make you cry.

11 **Which animals live on farms?**

○ elephants and hippos

○ birds and crocodiles

○ sheep and goats

12 **What does this story teach us about?**

○ what farmers do

○ how to grow crops

○ why people like oatmeal

13 **What do farmers need to do?**

    ○ eat a lot of corn and oatmeal

    ○ get up early in the morning

    ○ cook oatmeal for their family

14 **Why do farmers spend most of their time outside?**

    ○ Their crops and animals are outside.

    ○ They like eating their meals outside.

    ○ They do not like being inside.

Directions

Write your answer to Question B on the lines below. Base your answer on the two selections you have read.

B You read about Dan in "A Rainy Day" and about farmers in "A Farmer's Life." How do you think Dan would feel about spending a day outside on a farm? Tell why.

WRITING ACROSS TEXTS

_____

_ _

_____

_ _

_____

_ _

_____

_ _

_____

_ _

_____

_ _

_____

_ _

_____

_ _

_____

_ _

PART 2: HIGH-FREQUENCY WORDS

Directions

For Numbers 15 through 20, find the word that best fits in each sentence.

15 Kay liked to walk fast. She always got to school _____.

- ○ early
- ○ along
- ○ enough

16 We smell with our noses. We hear with our ears. We see with our _____.

- ○ kinds
- ○ goes
- ○ eyes

17 The teacher asked us if someone would help her. I _____, "I will!"

- ○ instead
- ○ answered
- ○ toward

18 Ted did not like the nuts. He asked for a _____ snack.

○ should

○ heavy

○ different

19 "My toy car broke," said Liz. "May I have _____ one?"

○ another

○ always

○ never

20 Bees are busy. They spend a lot of time flying _____ the flowers.

○ pulling

○ among

○ none

PART 3: PHONICS

Directions
For Numbers 21 through 34, find the answer to each question.

21 Which word is best in the sentence?
They used colored pens and _____.

○ paper

○ wagon

○ open

22 Dan said, "I want to go outside."
Which word has the same sound as the ou in outside?

○ your

○ through

○ count

23 Dan said, "I'm unhappy."
What has the same meaning as unhappy?

○ very happy

○ not happy

○ happy again

24 Joy and Dan didn't worry about the rain.
Which word rhymes with Joy?

○ jay

○ jar

○ toy

25 Joy asked

Do you know how to draw?

Which word rhymes with draw?

○ wait

○ saw

○ now

26 Which word makes the sentence correct?
Joy said, "I have always _____ drawing."

○ loved

○ lovd

○ lovved

27 Which word makes the sentence correct?
Joy and Dan were _____ colored pens.

○ ussing

○ useing

○ using

28 Farmers give people many different <u>kinds</u> of food.
Which word rhymes with <u>kinds</u>?

○ sends

○ finds

○ kids

29 Some <u>farmers</u> grow crops.
Which means the same as <u>farmers</u>?

○ people who work on farms

○ places where crops are grown

○ the biggest farms of all

30 They cook oatmeal and enjoy eating it with milk on top.
Which word is a compound word?

○ eating

○ enjoy

○ oatmeal

31 <u>Cows</u> give people milk.
Which word has the same sound as the <u>ow</u> in <u>cows</u>?

○ coat

○ low

○ how

GO ON

32 People also get meat from <u>cattle</u>.
How is the word <u>cattle</u> divided into syllables?

○ cat • tle

○ ca • ttle

○ catt • le

33 They spend <u>most</u> of their time outside among their crops and animals.
Which word rhymes with <u>most</u>?

○ cost

○ post

○ stop

34 You might be a <u>good</u> farmer.
Which word has the same sound as the <u>oo</u> in <u>good</u>?

○ book

○ cool

○ goat

PART 4: WRITING CONVENTIONS

Directions
Fill in the circle beside your answer choice for Numbers 35 through 40.

35 Which word makes the sentence correct?
Tom gave the ball to _____.

- ○ she
- ○ me
- ○ he

36 Which word makes the sentence correct?
_____ like to play in the park.

- ○ I
- ○ Me
- ○ Them

37 Which word makes the sentence correct?
First we ate lunch. _____ we rested.

- ○ Early
- ○ Next
- ○ Never

38 Which word makes the sentence correct?
When do _____ want to eat?

○ you

○ he

○ she

39 Which word makes the sentence correct?
Where do _____ go to school?

○ them

○ they

○ he

40 Which one is a command?

○ Do you go to school?

○ I have gone to school.

○ Go to school.

PROMPT

What do you like to do when you have free time? Do you like to be inside or outside? Why? Write at least three sentences to tell what you like to do when you have free time.

CHECKLIST FOR WRITERS

_____ Did I plan my paper before I started writing?

_____ Did I say why I like to be inside or outside?

_____ Did I say what I like to do when I have free time?

_____ Do my sentences make sense?

_____ Do my sentences begin with capital letters?

_____ Do my sentences end with end marks?

_____ Did I check my spelling?

_____ Did I make sure my paper is the way I want readers to read it?

NAME _____ DATE _____

Scott Foresman
Benchmark Test
End-of-Year

Reading STREET Grade 1

PEARSON

Glenview, Illinois
Boston, Massachusetts
Chandler, Arizona
Upper Saddle River, New Jersey

ISBN-13: 978-0-328-53729-7
ISBN-10:   0-328-53729-2
1 2 3 4 5 6 7 8 9 10 V016 19 18 17 16 15 14 13 12 11 10
CC1

ISBN-13: 978-0-328-53729-7
ISBN-10:   0-328-53729-2
EAN
9 780328 537297
90000>

Directions

Paco's favorite toy is missing! Read about how Paco's sister and mother look for the toy. Then answer Numbers 1 through 7.

Where Is Bear?

Rosa's little brother, Paco, had a favorite toy bear.

He took it every place he went.

One day Rosa's mother said, "I can't find Bear. I thought Bear was in Paco's bag. Now Bear isn't there. Paco will be very sad."

Rosa's mother said, "Rosa, I need your help to look for Bear. Let's think like detectives. Where are the places that Paco goes with Bear?"

Rosa answered, "Paco likes to sit with Bear in the playroom."

They looked there.

They didn't find Bear.

GO ON

Rosa thought some more.

Then she said, "Paco puts some of his toys in the toy box."

They looked through the toy box. There was no sign of Bear.

Then Rosa had another idea.

She went into Paco's room.

Benchmark Test   End-of-Year

She looked at Paco sleeping in his bed.

Right by his side was Bear.

Rosa ran to her mother and shouted, "I found Bear!"

When Rosa showed her mother where she found Bear, they both laughed.

Rosa's mother said, "You did a great job finding Bear. You are a wonderful detective."

GO ON

1 **Where were Rosa and her mother?**

- ○ in Paco's school
- ○ at their house
- ○ at the toy store

2 **At the end of the story, why did Rosa and her mother laugh?**

- ○ Paco had Bear the whole time.
- ○ Bear was in Paco's bag after all.
- ○ Paco told them a funny story.

3 **"Where Is Bear?" would be a make-believe story if**

- ○ Bear had been in the toy box.
- ○ Rosa had a little sister.
- ○ Bear could run and play.

4 **Which of these is best as another good name for this story?**

- ○ "Paco Is Sad"
- ○ "Rosa Finds Bear"
- ○ "Mother and Her Bear"

5 **Where did Paco like to sit with Bear?**

- ○ outside
- ○ in the playroom
- ○ at school

6 You can tell that Rosa was good at

○ playing ball.

○ hiding toys.

○ helping her mother.

7 What happened at the end of this story?

○ Rosa found Bear.

○ Rosa looked for Bear.

○ Rosa gave Bear to Paco.

The Hale Boys Build a Car

From the time they were two years old, the Hale brothers, Mike and Adam, loved cars.

When they were four, they were drawing cars on paper.

At age eight, they were making little toy cars from anything they could find around the house.

When they were ten, their father said, "Mike and Adam, you are old enough to build a car of your own. It can be big enough to ride in. I'll help you. We'll do it together."

They couldn't wait to get started!

GO ON

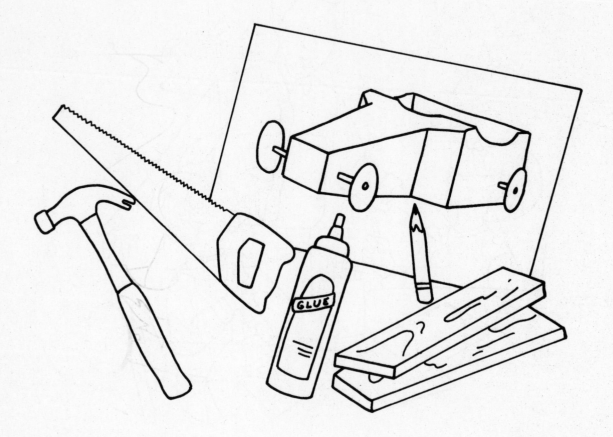

First, they drew the car on paper. They drew all the parts the car would have. Their father helped them.

Then their father said, "Now we can get the wood to make the car."

With their father's help, Mike and Adam used many tools to make the car. They were busy for weeks.

At last it was done. It was beautiful.

Their father took them to a big hill.

Mike and Adam got in the car. They raced down the hill.

The car worked! It was a great ride.

8 **What happened *first* in this story?**

○ Mike and Adam built a car.

○ Mike and Adam drew cars on paper.

○ The boys and their father got some wood.

9 **Which word best tells about the boys' father?**

○ silly

○ sad

○ nice

10 **Why did the boys' father let them build a car?**

○ He knew they loved cars.

○ He needed a new car.

○ He wanted the boys to play outside.

11 **What is this story mostly about?**

○ A boy shows his brother how to make a car.

○ Two brothers build a car with their father.

○ Two boys learn how to draw cars.

12 The author wanted you to

○ be happy for these boys.

○ know how to build cars.

○ learn all about cars.

13 How long were the boys busy building their car?

○ many days

○ many weeks

○ a few years

14 What is the big idea of the story?

○ If things don't work the first time, try again.

○ Not everything that works well has to look good.

○ You can make great things when you work together.

GO ON

Directions

Write your answer to Question A on the lines below. Base your answer on the two stories you have read.

A Think about what Rosa did in "Where Is Bear?" Think about what the father did in "The Hale Boys Build a Car." Tell how Rosa and the boys' father are alike.

WRITING
ACROSS
TEXTS

_____

- -

_____

- -

_____

- -

_____

- -

_____

- -

_____

- -

_____

- -

_____

Directions

Do you like horses? Read this to learn about riding a horse. Then answer Numbers 15 through 21.

Riding a Horse

Have you ever thought about riding a horse? There are good things about learning to ride a horse. You learn how to take care of an animal. And riding a horse is fun!

GO ON

Horses are larger than children. You must be big enough to stay on a horse before you learn to ride it. Some people can ride horses when they are six years old. Others must wait until they are eight.

Someone must teach you how to ride. People who know how to ride horses can show you how.

It's good to make friends with a horse before you ride it. Give the horse a snack. Pet the horse's head. Then you and the horse won't be afraid of each other.

First you will learn how to lead the horse around when you are not riding it. Then you will learn ways to get on the horse. After that, you are ready to ride it.

When you get older, you can learn to jump while riding.

If you get very good, later you can teach other people how to ride horses.

GO ON

15 Which of these statements is an opinion?

○ Some people can ride horses when they are six.

○ Horses are larger than children.

○ And riding a horse is fun!

16 When you are learning to ride a horse, what should you do first?

○ learn how to get on the horse

○ make friends with the horse

○ learn to jump while riding on the horse

17 Both the horse and the person learning to ride need to

○ trust each other.

○ be eight years old.

○ live on farms.

18 You should pet the horse before you ride it so that

○ the horse will sit down.

○ you can find the best horse to ride.

○ the horse will get to know you.

19 Making friends with a horse is most like

○ making a new friend at school.

○ getting to know a dog.

○ going to the zoo.

20 Right after you learn how to get on a horse, you can learn to

○ ride it.

○ jump with it.

○ lead it around.

21 The author wrote "Riding a Horse" to tell

○ how you learn to ride a horse.

○ how to take care of a horse.

○ why a horse makes a good pet.

Directions

Write your answer to Question B on the lines below. Base your answer on "The Hale Boys Build a Car" and "Riding a Horse."

B **Think about "The Hale Boys Build a Car" and "Riding a Horse." Would you rather build a car or ride a horse? Tell why.**

WRITING ACROSS TEXTS

_____

_____

_____

_____

_____

_____

_____

_____

_____

_____

PART 2: HIGH-FREQUENCY WORDS

Directions
Fill in the circle below your answer choice for Numbers 22 through 30.

22 "Where are you?" asked Tim. "I am over here," _____ Sue.

opened	loved	answered
○	○	○

23 Pam is going to have a birthday. She will be _____ years old.

above	eight	among
○	○	○

24 Bill said something funny. We all _____.

laughed	pulled	remembered
○	○	○

25 Mother made us a big dinner. We had _____ to eat.

enough	through	along
○	○	○

26 We went to the park today. There were many _____ there.

water	people	instead
○	○	○

GO ON

27 Matt had an idea. He _____ about the idea for a long time.

    touched   through   thought

      ○   ○   ○

28 We all like to play with Deb. She has many _____.

    friends   once   eyes

      ○   ○   ○

29 On the door we saw a _____. It said, "Come in."

    should   sign   science

      ○   ○   ○

30 Mike likes the zoo very much. He thinks all the animals
are _____.

    against   early   great

      ○   ○   ○

PART 3: PHONICS

Directions
For Numbers 31 through 51, mark the answer to each question.

31 Rosa looked in the <u>toy</u> box.
Which word has the same sound as the <u>oy</u> in <u>toy</u>?

       join   told   why
        ○   ○   ○

32 Paco was <u>sleeping</u> in his bed.
What is the base word of <u>sleeping</u>?

       pin   sleep   ping
        ○   ○   ○

33 Paco took his bear every <u>place</u> he went.
Which word rhymes with <u>place</u>?

       plan   catch   chase
        ○   ○   ○

34 At first they <u>didn't</u> find Bear.
What two words make up <u>didn't</u>?

      did not   does not   do not
        ○   ○   ○

GO ON

35 You will learn how to <u>lead</u> the horse around.
Which word has the same sound as the <u>ea</u> in <u>lead</u>?

bread	sleep	bed
○	○	○

36 <u>Later</u> you can teach other people how to ride horses.
How is the word <u>later</u> divided into syllables?

lat • er	late • r	la • ter
○	○	○

37 The brothers made cars from anything they found.
Which word in this sentence is a compound word?

brothers	anything	found
○	○	○

38 The boys <u>drew</u> cars on paper.
Which word has the same sound as the <u>ew</u> in <u>drew</u>?

saw	between	blue
○	○	○

39 Father helped the boys build a <u>big</u> car.
Which word means <u>the most big</u>?

bigful	biggest	bigger
○	○	○

40 They used <u>tools</u> to make a car.
Which word has the same sound as the <u>oo</u> in <u>tools</u>?

took ○   soon ○   told ○

41 The car raced <u>down</u> the hill.
Which word has the same sound as the <u>ow</u> in <u>down</u>?

know ○   boat ○   house ○

42 They could not <u>wait</u> to make their car.
Which word has the same sound as the <u>ai</u> in <u>wait</u>?

play ○   part ○   what ○

43 Rosa was a <u>wonderful</u> detective.
What is the base word of <u>wonderful</u>?

ful ○   wonder ○   won ○

44 People who <u>know</u> how to ride horses can show you how.
Which word has the same beginning sound as <u>know</u>?

snake ○   kite ○   need ○

45 Bear was <u>right</u> beside Paco.
Which word rhymes with <u>right</u>?

bite	list	fit
○	○	○

46 A person <u>shows</u> you how to ride.
Which word rhymes with <u>shows</u>?

stores	nose	cows
○	○	○

47 You may <u>teach</u> others to ride.
Which word means <u>a person who teaches</u>?

teaching	reteach	teacher
○	○	○

48 Pet the horse's <u>head</u>.
Which word has the same sound as the <u>ea</u> in <u>head</u>?

met	treat	street
○	○	○

49 When you get <u>older</u>, you can learn to jump.
Which words mean the same as <u>older</u>?

less old	more old	not old
○	○	○

50 It's good to make friends with the horse.
Which word has the same sound as the <u>oo</u> in <u>good</u>?

      boy   moon   book
      ○   ○   ○

51 Some people can ride horses when they are six years <u>old</u>.
Which word has the same sound as the <u>o</u> in <u>old</u>?

      most   cool   lost
      ○   ○   ○

STOP

PART 4: WRITING CONVENTIONS

Directions
Fill in the circle for your answer choice for Numbers 52 through 60.

52 Which sentence is written correctly?

○ Dinner Max wants.

○ Max wants to eat dinner.

○ Max dinner wants to.

53 We went to see a play on saturday.
Choose the word that should begin with a capital letter.

see	play	saturday
○	○	○

54 Mark the word that best fits in the sentence.
We _____ going to the park now.

are	were	is
○	○	○

55 Mark the word that best fits in the sentence.
They have the _____ house in the neighborhood.

smallest	smaller	less small
○	○	○

Benchmark Test   End-of-Year

56 Bob and Pat take a walk.
Which sentence means the same thing?

○ I take a walk.

○ We take a walk.

○ They take a walk.

57 Which sentence is written correctly?

○ Mary aren't at home today.

○ Mary isn't at home today.

○ Mary weren't at home today.

58 Which sentence is written correctly?

○ Bill saw I on the bus.

○ Bill saw she on the bus.

○ Bill saw her on the bus.

59 The fish swims around.
What word in the sentence is a noun?

fish   swims   around

○   ○   ○

60 The boy walked away.
What word in the sentence is a verb?

boy   walked   away

○   ○   ○

PART 5: WRITING

PROMPT

In "The Hale Boys Build a Car" and "Riding a Horse," children become old enough to do something new. Think about something new that you have learned to do this year. Write a story about a new thing you did this year. Tell how it made you feel.

CHECKLIST FOR WRITERS

_____ Did I plan my story before I started writing?

_____ Does my story tell about something new I learned to do this year?

_____ Does my story tell how doing something new made me feel?

_____ Does my story have a beginning, middle, and end?

_____ Does my story make sense?

_____ Do my sentences begin with capital letters?

_____ Do my sentences end with end marks?

_____ Did I check my spelling?

_____ Did I make sure my paper is the way I want readers to read it?